TRUST RISK Management

Assessing and Controlling Fiduciary Risk

Kenneth J. Namjestnik

BANKERS PUBLISHING COMPANY
PROBUS PUBLISHING COMPANY
Chicago, Illinois
Cambridge, England

ISBN 1-55738-327-8

Printed in the United States of America

BB

1 2 3 4 5 6 7 8 9 0

TABLE OF CONTENTS

Preface

This handbook is designed to provide trust management, trust compliance officers, auditors, and trust committees with a tool to properly assess and manage risks in the fiduciary services areas. We are not so blessed as to see an investment or business that actually yields a positive return without risk. It is everywhere there is a return to be made.

The management task is to control the risk consistent with the desired return. There are essentially two ways to control risk: 1) to control the "INHERENT RISK," i.e., the risk innately associated with a given product or service (for example, it is riskier to lend securities to brokers than to invest in U.S. T-Bills), and 2) to control the "RESIDUAL RISK," i.e., the risk left over after the decision is made to offer the product or provide the service (for example, if we choose to offer the securities lending product, we now have to control the credit risk of the broker, the bookkeeping risk of errors, the fidelity risk of possible diversion of securities, etc.).

After the controls are deftly put into place to control the residual risk (within a certain tolerance level), we now have a manageable risk. If the controls are not sufficient to make the risk manageable (the evaluation of which is usually provided by the internal or external auditor), we are left with "INTOLERABLE RISK." The audit steps used to independently evaluate the adequacy of the controls are covered in the **Trust Audit Manual** which can be used as a companion book to this publication. We will not duplicate that material here. We will focus here on assessing and managing the residual risk in the trust areas.

The format of this handbook is essentially by fiduciary business product lines (similar to the **Trust Audit Manual**). In Chapters 1 through 5, we discuss the residual risks associated with the management decision to accept new appointments and in the administration of the account along the following product lines:

Chapter 1   Personal Trust Administration

Chapter 2   Employee Benefit Trust Administration

Chapter 3   Corporate Bond Trustee and Agency Services

Chapter 4   Investment Portfolio Management and Collective Investment Funds

Chapter 5   Institutional Custody Services and Securities Lending

At the end of each chapter (with the exception of Chapter 5), there is a Fiduciary Compliance Risk Management Checklist which we have included to assist you in the management of compliance risk. Often, the laws and regulations will offer a level of protection in mitigating other risks as well. For example, in Chapter 1, the checklist includes regulatory aspects of proper account administration. By following the relevant regulation (in this case, 12CFR9.7), the bank can also mitigate the risks associated with lawsuits for breach of fiduciary duty, excessive expenses in defending itself against such litigation, competitive disadvantage from adverse publicity of the lawsuit, etc. We also believe the risk of noncompliance with laws and regulations can be potentially very large. For example, noncompliance can cause fines and surcharges, bad will with the regulatory agencies who might be responsible for approving future business activities, mergers, etc., and cease and desist orders over certain activities.

Chapter 6 includes operational and management risk issues, addressed from a management perspective, for the fiduciary services areas in general. This chapter approaches management risk issues from the standpoint of the economic, regulatory, and operational control climates surrounding trust activities. We hope this chapter will provide both food for thought and implementation tools for initiating and enhancing your risk management program.

Throughout the book, we have attempted to cover major risk elements that could lead to losses. Some of these include the following: errors in decision making, lost revenues, excessive expenses, destruction of assets, recordkeeping errors, fraud, competitive disadvantage, business interruption and, as mentioned above, violations of laws and regulations.

We have also included a number of appendices to serve as useful reference materials and to assist in managing risks. **Appendix A** includes the current version of the Office of the Comptroller of the Currency's, OCC, Risk Assessment Questionnaire which the OCC is using in the trust area as well as an interpretation of significant aspects of the questionnaire. This appendix spans all of the chapters of the handbook in its applicability. **Appendix B** provides a synopsis of the new risks imposed on corporate bond trustees by the Trust Indenture Reform Act of 1990. This appendix can be used as reference material for Chapter 3. **Appendix C** summarizes the investment ratings for various securities by the key ratings agencies use. This section will serve as a quick reference document for managing portfolio risk. It will also provide value in supplementing Chapter 4, "Portfolio Management." Finally, **Appendix D** includes a description of major policies which various offices of the Comptroller of the Currency have compiled to provide a tool in comparing against the policy coverage trust departments have in managing fiduciary risk.

We hope that this publication will provide you, your trust colleagues, and your institution with valuable, hands-on approaches to the management of risk in your fiduciary business services.

Acknowledgments

I would like to thank hundreds of people in the Fiduciary Services Industry for sharing their experiences over the years, which is what this book is all about—real fiduciary risk issues. My deepest thanks to you; you all know who you are.

My sincere thanks to Larry J. Musler who has some of the finest technical skills I have seen in the area of fiduciary compliance risk and how to minimize it. Larry contributed greatly in the conflict of interests policy issues.

Also, thanks to Ed Higgins, E.D. Higgins & Associates. Ed's dynamic and creative approach to the business and open-mindedness to many of my unique (to say the least) ideas over the years has been an inspiration to me.

Don Francis, thank you. Not only for your technical expertise on the OCC risk assessment issues, but for your perspective on all of the issues in this book and other things, great and small.

Finally, thanks to my family who love and tolerate me every day.

PERSONAL TRUST ADMINISTRATION

Personal trust provides professional trust administrative services for private individuals, families, or estates. Personal trust can provide a full range of trust services, including: safekeeping of assets, estate and tax planning, security cashiering, investment of assets, retirement planning, etc. When acting in the capacity of a fiduciary, a trust entity must act and invest following the "Prudent Man Rule" (in many states, effective 1991, there is a new "Prudent Investor Rule" adopted from the Third Restatement of Trusts). Often a trust department assumes great risk and exposure when an administrator is found to be acting without regard to this standard.

Within the personal trust division, there are often a number of products or relationships, including: living trusts, testamentary trusts, estate administration, guardianships for minors, conservatorships of incompetents, directed agency accounts, custodial accounts, and managing agency accounts. Each type of relationship

1

has its own set of rules and requires a certain level of skill and knowledge. For example, those "court accounts"—estate administration, guardianships, etc.—require a knowledge of court proceedings, schedules for accounting to the court, and knowledge of the state probate code for responsibilities, procedural issues and reporting requirements. Living or testamentary trusts may require a high proficiency in interpreting the trust agreement, determining that the dispositive provisions are met properly, etc.

The INHERENT RISKS in these products include the high level of regulatory sanctions involved, the complexity of administration of trusts, the requirement that investment management over these accounts be prudent, the expenses associated with the trust accounting system and its use, and the possibility that accounts and assets may be so complex in nature that the existing staff is not sufficiently skilled to administer the account without outside assistance. Since a fiduciary cannot delegate his or her fiduciary duties, the trust department would still be responsible to oversee the work of any outside agent brought in to assist in administration (e.g., outside real estate property management firm) and would continue to be responsible to the beneficiaries for any breaches of fiduciary duty.

Profitability of the trust department can be significantly impaired if the RESIDUAL RISKS associated with the decisions to accept new appointments and the administration of the accounts are not controlled properly.

DECISION TO ACCEPT NEW APPOINTMENT

Residual risks associated with the management decision of accepting a new personal trust appointment are as follows:

- Account administration needs are beyond the capability of existing staff.
- Assets to be delivered into the trust include assets that the trustee will have difficulty managing properly, e.g.,

real estate, closely-held business interests, mineral rights, etc.

- Environmental problems may exist with property being transferred to the trust, and the trustee may assume liability for the cost of cleanup and any fines.

- If the trustee does not review the instrument thoroughly, the instrument may be drafted to cause the trustee responsibility and liability beyond an acceptable level.

- Elements of the administration or assets being transferred may put the trustee in a conflict of interest situation.

- Fees quoted for the account may not be sufficient to assure that the account is reasonably profitable.

- Real estate located out of state may be subject to other statutes that the trustee is unfamiliar with.

- If the trust relationship is a successor trusteeship, the successor trustee may be exposed to liability for breach of fiduciary duty caused by the predecessor trustee if the successor has not taken steps to remedy the breach.

Controls to mitigate residual risk in accepting new personal trust appointments include the following:

- Proper training of senior trust officers and administrative support personnel in reviewing potential new business.

- Checklists to use in the review of the prospective account highlighting those areas of potential administration problems, operating support problems, conflicts of interest, unique asset administration beyond staff expertise, environmental problems, or legal or regulatory potential problems.

- Environmental studies over real estate which is intended to be conveyed into the trust.

- Review of the compensation in fees which would be chargeable to the account compared with the time required for administration and other activities.

- Determine if the trust is a successor relationship and, if so, why did the relationship terminate with the predecessor trustee. The account activity, tax filings, and other relevant information from the predecessor should be reviewed to ensure that there are no potential problems that could result in a loss to the bank as successor trustee.

- If there are assets intended to be delivered into the trust which the trustee deems unsuitable to meet the objectives of the trust, procedures should exist which assure that the assets are disposed of or the proper language exists in the trust to protect the trustee against liability for losses due to the continued retention of these assets.

ADMINISTRATION ACTIVITIES

Residual risks associated with the administration of personal trust accounts include the following:

- Not meeting the objectives of the trust due to lack of solid investment programs.

- Not meeting the objectives of the trust due to insufficient understanding of the provisions of the trust.

- Errors in the remittance of income to beneficiaries.

- Lack of documentation and potential for liability regarding discretionary decisions by the administrator.

- Untimely or improper investments in the account which cause the investments to fail to satisfy the trust objectives.

- Failing to satisfy the best interests of all beneficiaries when there are multiple beneficiaries with different objectives.

- Creating unacceptable customer relations if the beneficiaries' desires are contradictory to the duties of the trustee under the trust provisions.

- Failing to exercise required actions, e.g., payment of estimated taxes, income disbursements, principal distributions, and other actions because of inadequate tickler and monitoring systems.

- Incorrect preparation of tax returns due to inadequate recordkeeping or improper decisions or elections made by the trustee.

- Acting without obtaining proper approvals, for example, co-trustee approvals or committee approvals for discretionary distributions from the trust.

- Improper allocation of cash receipts to principal or income, due to insufficient understanding of state statute, insufficient understanding of the nature of the receipt, or lack of control over the posting of such receipts.

- Loss to the account from missing dividend payments, interest payments, capital change notifications (e.g., stock splits, etc.), due to insufficient accounting systems or lack of controls over payment monitoring and processing.

- Loss due to failing to meet sound fiduciary principles in the proper accounting to beneficiaries, safeguarding of assets, prudence, and caution in the account administration.

- Insufficient compensation due to errors in the fee computations, misjudging the level of administrative time required to manage the account, and excessive activity in the account compared with the fees, etc.

- Loss to the account for estate planning advice errors made by the trustee, e.g., unnecessary generation-skipping transfer tax imposed because of trustee counseling, power of appointment provision not executed due to poor monitoring by trustee, Q-Tip election not made by bank as executor under a will, etc.

■ Loss to the account due to poor cash management practices followed by the trustee.

■ Loss to the account due to the trustee retaining assets which it should have disposed of.

■ Excessive costs to the trustee because of ineffective or inefficient recordkeeping systems and/or continuous errors in the records.

■ Imprudent practices such as allowing brokers to hold securities for the trust in their street name and subsequently lending out those securities.

Controls to mitigate residual risk in administration activities include the following:

■ Clearly defined investment strategies in marketable securities, including asset allocation models for the accounts based upon the account objectives.

■ Proper account setup procedures, including all relevant tickler information for remittances, accountings to interested parties, estimated tax payments, birthdays and anniversaries which may trigger trustee actions, etc.

■ Procedures to assure that contributions to the account are invested in a timely manner, cash awaiting investment or distribution is properly made productive through the use of sweep systems, and the account is monitored for overdraft situations which would cause loss to the bank in the form of an interest free loan.

■ Account reviews are held at least annually to assure that the account is being properly administered, the assets are suitable to meet the objectives of the account, and all tickled events have been properly acted upon.

- Procedures to ensure that where there is an outside powerholder, e.g., a co-trustee, any instructions are properly documented in writing and instructions are only acted upon if the proper power is ascertained.

- Where the trustee has the power to exercise discretion in distributing principal or income of the trust, procedures should exist to ensure that the trustee has made his or her discretionary decision prudently upon all of the facts and circumstances surrounding the decision. A discretionary committee might be employed to approve all discretionary distributions after proper review of the request for distribution against the relevant allowing provisions of the instrument.

- When an administrative task is delegated to an outside agent, procedures should exist for the proper oversight and supervision of the outside agent's activities to ensure satisfactory performance.

- Procedures to document actions of the trustee should incorporate filing methods and locations, retention schedules, and minimum standards of documentation for all actions, such as: discretionary distributions, discretionary investment of funds (including a clear trail of the account objectives to the investment objectives and the resulting investments), criteria for various tax elections, meetings with the beneficiaries or principals in agency accounts, and minutes of court proceedings and court accountings.

- Procedures to make certain that personal and real tangible property is adequately insured if the trustee deems it prudent to insure against loss.

- Procedures to insure that adequate compensation is collected from the accounts, including management approvals (reviewed annually), of any fee concessions from the standard fee schedule.

- Procedures to insure that proper actions are taken when a beneficiary's (or principal's) directive is contradictory to the provisions of the trust (or agency contract).

FIDUCIARY COMPLIANCE RISK MANAGEMENT CHECKLIST

COMPLIANCE PROGRAM _____   Check, WP Ref.

or Initials

NUMBER _____ AS OF DATE _____

CASH MANAGEMENT PRACTICES (12CFR9.10(a))

1. Synoptic: Requires bank to formulate policies and procedures to ensure the proper investment of funds (cash) awaiting investment or distribution. Further, policies and procedures must ensure that the fiduciary account receives the maximum rate of return available for trust quality or short-term investments.

2. Policy(ies)/Procedure(s): Should address the quality of the short-term vehicle to be used for making fiduciary funds productive; the frequency of "sweeping" the fiduciary funds to the short-term vehicle; the "floor" for sweeping (recommended to be swept to $.00); and the criteria used for using any "in-bank" investment vehicles to prevent self-dealing situations.

3. Related Bank Policies:

4. Related Issues:

   a. Banks have been forced to surcharge them-
   selves by the Office of the Comptroller of the
   Currency, OCC, for failure to follow sound fiduciary principles in making fiduciary cash productive (Scott on Trusts Sec. 180.3—Duty to Make
   Cash Productive).

   b. Fiduciary cash has been interpreted by the OCC
   as cash in any account where the bank has discretion in whether to invest the cash and/or in
   what vehicle to invest it.

   c. Banks have unsuccessfully defended class action litigation against a "floor" below which the
   cash was not made productive. This was the
   case even though the bank argued that the
   costs to invest below this floor were in excess of
   the imputed value to the client.

   d. Sweep fees (*see* Conflicts of Interest).

FIDUCIARY COMPLIANCE RISK MANAGEMENT CHECKLIST

COMPLIANCE PROGRAM _____ Check, WP Ref.

or Initials

NUMBER _____ AS OF DATE _____

CASH MANAGEMENT PRACTICES (12CFR9.10(b))

1. Synoptic: Cash deposited in own national bank fiduciary accounts must be collateralized with bank assets. This is a requirement of this regulation as promulgated by 12USC92a(d). The fiduciary funds that are pledgable must be in excess of FDIC insurance, and nonfiduciary funds are not pledgable since "earmarking" general bank assets must be done in accordance with the Uniform Commercial Code and Bankruptcy Statutes relating to preferential treatment of various classes of creditors. Therefore, 12USC92a(d) is both a directive AND an allowing statute.

2. Policy(ies)/Procedure(s): Should address the identification of accounts subject to pledging requirement; determination of amount to be pledged; and securities classes eligible for pledging (see P&Os 9.2700-9.2740 for amount subject to pledge and eligible securities to pledge).

3. Related Bank Policies:

4. Related Issues:

   a. Bank Interpretive Letter 464 opines that national banks lack the authority to pledge their own assets for the fiduciary funds of an affiliate. (There are some allowing statutes at state level.) State banks may have different pledging requirements under relevant state statutes, e.g., pledging based upon fiduciary assets managed. Some states also require pledging of bank assets for court-supervised fiduciary accounts, e.g., estates, conservatorships, guardianships, etc. Regulation 12CFR9.14 provides that national banks make the same relevant pledges for these purposes as state-chartered banks are required to under state statute.

   b. P&Os 9.3100-9.3117 re: funds awaiting investment or distribution.

FIDUCIARY COMPLIANCE RISK MANAGEMENT CHECKLIST

COMPLIANCE PROGRAM _____   Check, WP Ref.

or Initials

NUMBER _____ AS OF DATE _____

ADMINISTRATION OF FIDUCIARY POWERS
(12CFR9.7(a)(1))

1. Synoptic: Requires the board of directors to be responsible for the exercise of fiduciary powers. The
   board may assign the day-to-day responsibility for
   the execution of these powers to committees or appropriate, responsible officers, but may not delegate
   the responsibility of acting in accordance with
   sound, fiduciary principles to these individuals. Any
   assignment of the duties of execution should be
   duly noted, through resolution, in the minutes of the
   board meetings and, if further assigned by an
   authoritative committee, should be duly noted in
   such committee's meeting minutes.

2. Policy(ies)/Procedure(s): Should address the oversight mechanism between the board and the responsible committees or individuals who have been
   granted the authority to execute the activities necessary to carry out the bank's fiduciary duties under
   its trust powers.

3. Related Bank Policies:

4. Related Issues:

  a. P&Os 9.1090-9.1390 related to supervision.

  b. "Sound fiduciary principles": Scott on Trusts Section 170 Duty of Loyalty; Section 172 Duty to Keep and Render Accounts; Section 179 Duty to Keep Trust Property Separate; Section 227 Investments which a Trustee Can Properly Make (Prudent Investor Rule); and Section 230 Duty to Dispose of Improper Investments.

FIDUCIARY COMPLIANCE RISK MANAGEMENT CHECKLIST

COMPLIANCE PROGRAM_____   Check, WP Ref.

or Initials

NUMBER _____ AS OF DATE _____

ADMINISTRATION OF FIDUCIARY POWERS (12CFR9.7(a)(2))

1. Synoptic: Requires prior approval of board or their designates prior to acceptance of fiduciary accounts. Additionally, requires written record of acceptance and termination of all fiduciary accounts. A prompt review (60 days under P&O 9.4103) needs to be conducted to determine if any assets delivered are unsuitable and to determine how to dispose of them and to establish an investment program for the account. This section also requires an annual account review to be performed each calendar year and within 15 months from the prior review. (P&O 9.4102 requires BOTH an asset review by issuer as well as an individual account review by account.)

2. Policy(ies)/Procedure(s): Should address initial account acceptance process, including criteria to be evaluated; issuer and account review standards, including approval processes for retention and sale of assets and supporting documentation; real estate, closely held businesses, and other "specialized" or less-than-readily-marketable assets as well as marketable securities.

3. Related Bank Policies:

4. Related Issues:

   a. P&Os 9.4000-9.4070 re: investments

   b. P&Os 9.4100-9.4120 re: asset and account reviews

   c. P&O 9.4230 re: options contracts

   d. P&O 9.4305-9.4310 re: brokers and dealers

   e. P&O 9.4400 re: excessive trading

   f. Trust Banking Circulars 2 (options), 4 (mutual funds), 14 (futures), 22 (repurchase agreements)

FIDUCIARY COMPLIANCE RISK MANAGEMENT CHECKLIST

COMPLIANCE PROGRAM _____   Check, WP Ref.

or Initials

NUMBER _____ AS OF DATE _____

ADMINISTRATION OF FIDUCIARY POWERS
(12CFR9.7(b)-(c))

1. Synoptic: Section (b) requires that all officers and employees of the trust department be bonded, and section (c) requires that the bank employ or retain legal counsel to them on fiduciary matters.

2. Policy(ies)/Procedure(s): Should address both the bonding of employees and the retention of fiduciary legal counsel.

3. Related Bank Policies:

4. Related Issues:

FIDUCIARY COMPLIANCE RISK MANAGEMENT CHECKLIST

COMPLIANCE PROGRAM _____   Check, WP Ref.

or Initials

NUMBER _____ AS OF DATE _____

ADMINISTRATION OF FIDUCIARY POWERS (12CFR9.7(d))

1. Synoptic: Requires national banks to establish written policies and procedures to prohibit using "nonpublic" information when making investment decisions in the trust department. This is often referred to as the "Chinese Wall" and is intended to guard against violation of the Anti-Fraud provisions of the Securities Exchange Act of 1934 (Rule 10b-5).

2. Policy(ies)/Procedure(s): Should address the prohibition of using material inside information to trade securities; specifically, should address nonpublic information contained in the commercial loan area, corporate trust area or anywhere within the bank or obtained from outside sources which could influence the trust department's decision to buy or sell securities of the company in question. Confidentiality of such information is of paramount importance.

3. Related Bank Policies:

4. Related Issues:

   a. Rule 10b-5 Anti-Fraud provisions of Securities Exchange Act of 1934.

FIDUCIARY COMPLIANCE RISK MANAGEMENT CHECKLIST

COMPLIANCE PROGRAM _____   Check, WP Ref.

or Initials

NUMBER _____ AS OF DATE _____

SPECIAL ASSET ADMINISTRATION
(OPTIONS CONTRACTS)

1. Synoptic: Trust Banking Circular 2 governs the use
    of options contracts for fiduciary accounts. It re-
    quires the opinion of bank counsel for the permissi-
    bility under local law, specific policies and
    procedures approved by the board or its designee
    prior to using options, sufficiently detailed record-
    keeping systems, compliance with Options Clearing
    Corporation standards for escrow receipts, clarity of
    investment strategy to distinguish from speculative
    use of such contracts, daily mark to market of the
    contracts and internal controls which are adequate
    to: 1) monitor market prices of the options, the un-
    derlying securities, and the expiration of the con-
    tracts; 2) assure compliance with Federal Reserve
    regulations on option contract margin and settle-
    ment procedures; and 3) assure settlement reports
    are reconciled to the trades by someone other than
    the person executing the transaction.

2. Policy(ies)/Procedure(s): Required by this circular to
    define permissible option strategies, e.g., only cov-
    ered call options should be reviewed annually. Addi-
    tionally, the policies and procedures should address
    the internal control, accounting, and monitoring pro-
    cedures noted above.

3. Related Bank Policies:

4. Related Issues:
    a. P&O 9.4230 on option guarantee letters; 12CFR9.11 Investment of Funds Held as Fiduciary.

FIDUCIARY COMPLIANCE RISK MANAGEMENT CHECKLIST

COMPLIANCE PROGRAM _____   Check, WP Ref.

or Initials

NUMBER _____ AS OF DATE _____

SPECIAL ASSET ADMINISTRATION (MUTUAL FUNDS)

1. Synoptic: Trust Banking Circular 4 allows investments in mutual funds if the following exists: 1) authority in state statute or decisions, 2) specific authority in the appropriate governing instrument, or 3) binding consents from all beneficiaries. These investments must also be appropriate for the accounts involved. Prudence and suitability remain the key issues as to the investment itself.

2. Policy(ies)/Procedure(s): Should address the holding of mutual funds, including retention of mutual funds delivered in kind to the trust and the method for monitoring their continued use in an account. Policy should also address use of funds which the bank advises, 12b-1 funds, and funds that offer the bank a financial benefit for steering discretionary money into such funds.

3. Related Bank Policies:

4. Related Issues:

   a. P&O 9.3910 re: prohibition of using 12b-1 funds
   for fiduciary accounts, P&O 9.3116 re: use of
   mutual funds advised by the bank ("private la-
   bel" funds), Banking Circular 233 re: acceptance
   of financial benefits from fund sponsors;
   12CFR9.11 Investment of Funds Held as Fiduciary; Trust Interpretive Letter 234 prohibiting use
   of bank-advised mutual funds for fiduciary accounts where bank receives an advisory fee;
   Bank Interpretive Letter 558 supporting TIL 234.

FIDUCIARY COMPLIANCE RISK MANAGEMENT CHECKLIST

COMPLIANCE PROGRAM _____ Check, WP Ref.

or Initials

NUMBER _____ AS OF DATE _____

SPECIAL ASSET ADMINISTRATION
(CLOSELY HELD BUSINESSES)

1. Synoptic: Many closely held businesses become fiduciary assets by means of their inclusion in a decedent's estate. The executor, under the will, distributes the business from the estate into a trust. The bank, as trustee, may be a controlling or minority shareholder. The bank must assess the best interests of the beneficiaries in determining whether to retain the business in trust or to sell the business and should consider the following factors: a) financial condition of the company, b) quality and succession of management, c) earnings potential, d) growth potential and estimated life of the business, e) marketability of the business if sale is recommended, f) product or service line profitability, and g) competition in this industry. The best interests of the beneficiaries are often served by having a bank officer sit on the board of the company to direct policy. Naturally, D&O liability insurance should be secured for these board members to minimize losses to the officer, the trust, and the bank in the event of litigation.

---

2. Policy(ies)/Procedure(s): Should address acceptance and ongoing administration of closely held businesses addressing the best interests of the beneficiaries.

3. Related Bank Policies:

4. Related Issues:

    a. *OCC Handbook for Fiduciary Activities*, p. 33;
       P&Os 9.2955 re: fees from serving as director
       and 9.3895 re: use of bank credit for closely
       held businesses; 12CFR9.11 Investment of
       Funds Held as Fiduciary.

FIDUCIARY COMPLIANCE RISK MANAGEMENT CHECKLIST

COMPLIANCE PROGRAM _____   Check, WP Ref.

or Initials

NUMBER _____ AS OF DATE _____

SPECIAL ASSET ADMINISTRATION (REAL ESTATE)

1. Synoptic: Real estate may represent a significant investment holding in many trusts. The real estate may be delivered in kind to the trust or purchased as an investment by the trustee. The trustee should consider the following factors in decisions to purchase, retain, or sell the real estate property: a) authority to purchase in the governing instrument, b) if leased, quality of lease and tenants, c) future marketability of property, d) assessment of risk factors, including environmental liability, e) investment yields, f) current appraisals of market value, g) cash flow, potential for appreciation, and tax benefits, and h) suitability for the given account. For agricultural, commercial, ranch, and other special management type property, the trustee should further consider the skill levels required to properly manage the property and compare the requirements to its ability to manage the property through its own departments or through management agents. (The fiduciary responsibility, however, cannot be delegated to such agents.)

2. Policy(ies)/Procedure(s): Should address the acceptance process of real estate being delivered into a trust, the investment standards for purchase, the process to review suitability, the appraisal process, the hiring of outside agents, and the review for environmental issues.

3. Related Bank Policies:

4. Related Issues:

a. 12CFR9.11 Investment of Funds Held as Fiduciary; P&Os 9.1090 re: engagement in real estate
activities; 9.3890 re: use of other service areas
of bank for real estate activities; 9.3900 re:
transactions with related parties; 9.4120 re: real
estate inspections and appraisals; and *OCC
Handbook for Fiduciary Activities,* pp. 36-37.

FIDUCIARY COMPLIANCE RISK MANAGEMENT CHECKLIST

COMPLIANCE PROGRAM_____ Check, WP Ref.

or Initials

NUMBER _____ AS OF DATE _____

SPECIAL ASSET ADMINISTRATION
(MISCELLANEOUS ASSETS)

1. Synoptic: Assets such as restricted securities, mineral interests, partnerships, tangibles (e.g., coin collections), private placements, loans, repurchase agreements, forward futures contracts, et al., offer special concerns to fiduciaries. These types of assets are often delivered in kind. The trustee's responsibility to determine their suitability and legality in the relevant account is determined by the terms of the instrument, common law duties, court order, or local law. Each of these types of assets has a degree of nonmarketability associated with it, and its holding must be determined as prudent for the account where the trustee has been determined as responsible for the asset.

2. Policy(ies)/Procedure(s): Should address the investment and retention decisions involved with these types of nonmarketable securities assets, as well as the level of supporting documentation required for decisions to invest, retain, or sell.

3. Related Bank Policies:

4. Related Issues:

    a. Restricted and control securities disclosure re-
       quirements under Rule 144; holding of general
       partnership assets may expose bank to unlim-
       ited liability unless limited by local law; repur-
       chase agreements subject to TBC 22; forward
       futures contracts subject to TBC 14; 12CFR9.11
       Investment of Funds Held as Fiduciary; P&Os
       9.4070 re: speculative investments; 9.4025 re:
       SBA loans; *OCC Handbook for Fiduciary Activi-
       ties*, pp. 41-44.

CHAPTER TWO

EMPLOYEE BENEFIT TRUST ADMINISTRATION

This growing product continues to be an important source of revenue for trust departments. As trustee, the bank provides professional trust services for corporate, public, partnership, sole proprietorship, and union qualified and nonqualified employee benefit plans. These services can include the following: custody and safekeeping of assets, security settlements, benefit payments, payment of expenses, preparation of reports, annual accounting, tax withholding and tax filings, and investment management.

The types of plans that the trust department acts as trustee upon vary widely. They can include: 1) qualified defined benefit pension plans; 2) qualified defined contribution plans (including: a) profit sharing plans, b) money purchase plans, c) 401(k) cash or deferred arrangements, d) employee stock ownership (ESOP) plans, e) simplified employee pension plans (SEPPs), f) thrift plans, g) stock bonus plans); 3) tax deferred annuity arrangements; 4) nonqualified government plans; 5) nonqualified top-hat plans (often with rabbi trusts); 6) welfare benefit plans such as flexible spending accounts; and others.

It is probably quite clear from the variety of available benefit plans that the CAPABILITY OF STAFF is an important ingredient in the risk management in offering these products. Proper staff training is crucial to a successful trust relationship. The LEVEL OF REGULATORY SANCTIONS, particularly compliance with the Employee Retirement Income Security Act (ERISA) of 1974 and the Internal Revenue Code, also bear upon the inherent risk of offering this product.

Also, banks have different services for each of the plans. The services include: 1) trusteeship with investment responsibility; 2) directed trusteeship with investment management performed by an outside registered investment advisor; 3) agent and/or custodian only; 4) plan administrator (although this responsibility is an extremely high level responsibility with a lot of liability; many banks offer administration services if the employer is not equipped to administer the plan); 5) participant recordkeeper; and 6) collective fund manager. Each of these relationships varies in the element of inherent risk the service has within it. The bank must understand the inherent risk in each of the relationships it enters into.

DECISION TO ACCEPT NEW APPOINTMENT

Residual risks associated with the management decision to accept a new employee benefit account appointment include the following:

- Responsibilities under the plan and trust are not clearly identified, including responsibilities for plan administration tasks (e.g., discrimination testing, meeting vesting, minimum participation and other requirements of the Internal Revenue Code for Plan Qualification, preparation of Summary Plan Descriptions, etc.), investment management (unless an outside Registered Investment Advisor has been appointed and has acknowledged his or her role as a plan fiduciary), actuarial calculations for defined benefit plans, etc.

- If the plan is already in existence, records at both the plan and participant levels may not provide adequate information of past activities or whether the IRS has issued a favorable determination letter as to the plan's qualified status.

- Plan assets may include assets of the employer or another party in interest which might indicate that there have been one or more prohibited transactions involving the plan.

- The bank may be taking on more duties and responsibilities than it has the capacity for in terms of personnel and operating systems support.

- As there is wide variety in the types of benefit plans and the required recordkeeping necessary to properly administer the plans, participant recordkeeping systems may not be sufficient to handle the type of plan being accepted.

- Fees may not be sufficient to make the account relationship reasonably profitable.

- Assets held in the plan (if already in existence) may create issues that expose the bank to potential liability in such activities as proxy voting, or if they are investments in companies that are politically or socially sensitive, they may offend the general public and society or cause embarrassment to the bank.

- The plan may not be structured to qualify for favorable tax treatment or the plan may be poorly structured such that the employer will not be able to meet the financial requirements for funding. This could cause administrative nightmares down the road in dealing with the Pension Benefit Guaranty Corporation, litigation by participants, etc.

Controls to mitigate residual risk in accepting new employee benefit administration accounts include the following:

- Policies, procedures, and new account checklists to identify responsibilities and potential prohibited transactions, recognize imprudence in investments, and indicate the type of plan and the qualification requirements for the plan to test against the plan document.

- Policies that identify the types of plans that will be accepted, not accepted, and the various relationships that will be accepted (e.g., trustee, custodian only, etc.) for each type of plan being considered.

- Procedures to identify any potential conflict of interest situations, including statutory prohibited transactions.

- Management approval procedures, including specificity on the responsibilities the trust department will be assuming, e.g., investment manager if there is not a registered investment advisor to the plan that has acknowledged in writing his or her role as a plan fiduciary; plan administrator for those accounts which use the trust department to perform plan administrator tasks or where the trust department has a prototype plan for which it is responsible in obtaining favorable IRS determination letters, etc.

- Procedures to review for special activities and risks, e.g., participant loan provisions and the responsibilities of the trust department in administering these loan programs; 401(k) plans and the associated tests of deferral percentages ("ADP Testing") unique to these plans; ESOPs, particularly those for closely held businesses where the trustee has risks associated with voting of proxies, valuation of the securities, leveraged funding of the ESOP, etc.

- Procedures to identify if the needs of the plan can be satisfied by the investment strategies and objectives currently employed by the bank or whether the plan administrator requires specialized investment skills, e.g., the use of index futures, foreign investments, etc.

- Procedures which incorporate a full checklist of documentation required, i.e., employee lists, tax filings, spousal consents, retirees eligible for distributions, summary plan descriptions, participant directed investment plans, etc.

- Policies which assure the proper level of expertise through appropriate employee benefit plan (EBP) training, ERISA compliance training, adequate library of administration forms and checklists, IRS regulations library, and subscriptions to appropriate publications and periodicals.

ADMINISTRATION ACTIVITIES

Residual risks associated with the administration of employee benefit accounts include the following:

- Improper or untimely responses to plan administrator or participant requests for information.

- Improper or untimely preparation of required documents, forms, and tax filings, e.g., preparation of summary plan descriptions or material modifications to the plan; 1099 reporting to plan participants receiving distributions; required reporting to recipients of lump sum distributions; preparation of Form 5500 or the related certifications to the plan administrator if they are filing Form 5500; preparation and processing of requests for loans and obtaining spousal consents; preparation of participants' accountings; required notification to allow participants to change their investment mix if the plan includes a participant-directed investment feature.

- Receipt of unauthorized directions or directions that are not evidenced in writing from the plan administrator, participants, beneficiaries, investment advisors, actuaries, or other interested parties.

- Untimely or improper deposits of funds from the employer or employee causing the funds to go uninvested.

- Violations of the plan provisions, ERISA, IRS regulations, etc., for example, allowing the purchase of employer assets by the plan (if not qualifying employer real estate or securities); allowing more than the allowable contributions by an employee or the employer, thereby jeopardizing plan qualification or causing the contribution to be taxable; allowing excessive distributions from the plan, thereby creating an excise tax on such excess distribution; allowing a plan loan without obtaining spousal consent, thereby violating the Retirement Equity Act of 1984 and creating liability for the plan to the spouse, etc.

- Failure to satisfy the Prudent Investor Rule of ERISA by not properly diversifying plan assets or not keeping the indicia of ownership of plan assets within the jurisdiction of the U.S. district courts.

- Failure to act in the best interests of participants and beneficiaries in the voting of proxies.

- Commingling the assets of qualified plans with other accounts in a pooled fund which may cause the fund to lose its tax exempt status under Revenue Ruling 81-100 or cause the fund to have to be registered under the Investment Company Act of 1940.

Controls to mitigate residual risk associated with the administration of employee benefit accounts include the following:

- Policies and procedures which set forth standards in responding to authorized interested parties regarding administration issues.

- Checklists to control the timeliness and accuracy of preparation and processing of required information, e.g., ticklers for Form 5500 preparation; 1099 reporting; preparation and distribution of summary plan descriptions and material modifications to the plan; plan loan administration checklists; ticklers for anticipating receipt of contributions to the plan; checklists for distributing required documents to terminating employees, retiring employees, and the like; checklists to control required employee information for new hires by the employer, new participants to the plan, "rollovers" to the plan from other plans (if the plan allows for such), etc.

- Checklists to determine who is a party in interest under ERISA definitions in order to properly monitor for prohibited transactions.

- Procedures which require checking contribution limits and distribution limits (including the tax deferral limits for 401(k) plans), either manually or through an automated participant recordkeeping system, to assure there are no violations of these limits.

- Procedures which require written instructions or written confirmations of verbal instructions (e.g., within 48 hours) to prevent against unauthorized instructions or the inability to support an action later if questioned or contradicted by a participant or relevant authorized party.

- Policies and procedures to review the assets of the trust under the plan, at least annually, to ascertain if the objectives of the plan (or the fund into which plan assets are invested) are being met.

- Policies and procedures regarding the voting of proxies to assure the voting is always in the best interests of the plan participants and their beneficiaries.

- Procedures to ensure that all plan assets have a documented, objective market value associated with them to ensure the proper distribution to terminating or retiring employees.

- Policies regarding the preservation of qualified plan status and the level of expertise required by the staff to ensure the plan does not lose its qualification.

ADDITIONAL INVESTMENT RISK ISSUES

When investing funds for employee benefit clients, the following additional risks also must be addressed:

- Diversification standards of ERISA Section 404
- Investing in securities not allowed by the plan document or trust agreement
- Improper delegation of powers
- Improper and/or unauthorized directives
- Failure to comply with ERISA's "Prudent Investor" rule
- Fails, overdrafts, and cash advances
- Insider trading and other regulatory restrictions
- Failure to invest single purpose accounts properly, e.g., company stock funds
- Proxy voting in accordance with the best interests of the participants and beneficiaries

The employee benefit area needs to be aware of the types of risk faced by their customers, who by the nature of their benefit programs, require different levels of risk in their investment portfolios. These risks can change according to the type of account, i.e., corporate clients (private or public), public funds, or Taft-Hartley Act (collectively bargained) plans. Some additional risks include the following:

- Improper risk management levels for the plan
- Untimely receipt of trade instructions from outside registered investment advisors
- Opportunity risk
- Credit or default risk
- Nonexecution or nonavailability of the proper investment product in the market

As employee benefit departments stretch to keep up with increasing demand for employee benefit trust services, the potential for liability also increases. As the department expands, so must the department's knowledge and resources. Multiple investment managers, real estate funds, FNMAs, CMOs, etc., force the plan administrator to become an expert in a greater number of areas, in turn increasing possible exposure to the following economic risks within the investment function:

- Money supply fluctuations
- Interest rates
- Inflationary pressures and concerns
- Inability to properly anticipate the actions of the Federal Reserve Board
- Responsiveness of the global securities market
- The volume and types of new security issues brought to the market

FIDUCIARY COMPLIANCE RISK MANAGEMENT CHECKLIST

COMPLIANCE PROGRAM_____   Check, WP Ref.

or Initials

NUMBER _____ AS OF DATE _____

ERISA (SECTION 404)

1. Synoptic: Section 404 was updated in 1991 by the DOL to include Section 404(c) regarding relief from fiduciary duty rules when participants direct their own investments under certain conditions. Generally, Section 404 sets out the duties of a fiduciary under ERISA for diversification of assets, acting solely in the best interests of participants, maintaining the indicia of ownership of plan assets within the jurisdiction of the U.S. district courts, and other rules. Banks, exempt from registration as registered investment advisors under the Investment Advisors Act of 1940, will have fiduciary responsibilities for investments unless there is a registered investment advisor appointed in the plan documents (or in a separate appointment by the plan fiduciary) who has acknowledged his or her role as a plan fiduciary in writing (ERISA 3(38)).

2. Policy(ies)/Procedure(s): Should address specific actions that the bank will take to carry out its fiduciary responsibilities under ERISA to protect plan participants, e.g., prohibited transaction monitoring, remedying co-fiduciary breaches of duty, etc. Should also address its responsibilities for investment management when there is a named registered investment advisor.

3. Related Bank Policies:

4. Related Issues:

FIDUCIARY COMPLIANCE RISK MANAGEMENT CHECKLIST

COMPLIANCE PROGRAM _____   Check, WP Ref.

or Initials

NUMBER _____ AS OF DATE _____

ERISA (SECTION 402)

1. Synoptic: Section 402 requires that every employee benefit plan be established and maintained in writing and provide for one or more named fiduciaries who will have authority to control and manage the operation and administration of the plan. The plan must describe any procedure for the allocation of responsibilities for the operation and administration of the plan, and the plan may provide that a named fiduciary may employ one or more persons to render advice (e.g., investment advice) with regard to any responsibility such fiduciary has under the plan.

2. Policy(ies)/Procedure(s): Should address the proper authorities for appointment or employment of anyone who will render advice or perform functions under the plan. Specifically, the appointment of an outside registered investment advisor to the plan should include a procedure to document that the advisor is registered by getting a certification from such advisor as well as a statement acknowledging that advisor's role as a plan fiduciary.

3. Related Bank Policies:

4. Related Issues:

FIDUCIARY COMPLIANCE RISK MANAGEMENT CHECKLIST

COMPLIANCE PROGRAM _____ Check, WP Ref.

or Initials

NUMBER _____ AS OF DATE _____

ERISA (SECTION 405)

1. Synoptic: Section 405 discusses the liability a plan fiduciary has under ERISA for breaches of a co-fiduciary. Essentially, he or she is liable if: a) he or she participates knowingly in or knowingly undertakes to conceal an act or omission by a fiduciary, knowing such act or omission is a breach; b) by his or her failure to comply with the fiduciary duty provisions of Section 404, he or she has enabled such other fiduciary to commit a breach; or c) he or she has knowledge of a co-fiduciary breach without making reasonable efforts under the circumstances to remedy the breach.

2. Policy(ies)/Procedure(s): Should address the fiduciary's duties to act solely in the best interests of the participants and beneficiaries under the standards imposed under Section 404; it also should include the actions the fiduciary will take should a co-fiduciary breach become known through the fiduciary's carrying out of his or her own fiduciary duties. It is important to consider, in any policies, that the fiduciary may be jointly or severally liable depending somewhat on the plan document, the prior actions of the fiduciary, and whether the fiduciary knew (or reasonably should have known in the carrying out of his or her own fiduciary duties) of the breach.

3. Related Bank Policies:

4. Related Issues:

FIDUCIARY COMPLIANCE RISK MANAGEMENT CHECKLIST

COMPLIANCE PROGRAM _____ Check, WP Ref.

or Initials

NUMBER _____ AS OF DATE _____

ERISA (SECTION 406)

1. Synoptic: Section 406 sets out transactions that are prohibited under ERISA. Essentially, it states that a fiduciary shall not cause the plan to engage in: a) sales, exchanges, or leases of property, b) loans or other extensions of credit, c) furnishing of goods or services, d) transfers of assets between the plan and a "party in interest" (as defined in Section 3(14) of ERISA). It also prohibits plan acquisition of employer securities or employer real property except as provided in ERISA Section 407. It goes on to say that a fiduciary: a) shall not deal with the plan assets in his or her own interest, b) shall not act in any transaction on behalf of a party whose interests are adverse to the plan's or participant's interests, or c) shall not receive any consideration for his or her own personal account from any party dealing with such plan in connection with a transaction involving the assets of the plan.

2. Policy(ies)/Procedure(s): Should address the monitoring of prohibited transactions by identifying parties in interest to the plan and prohibiting the transaction types described in this section between the plan and such parties; should further address potential self-dealing issues such as: sweep fees, soft-dollar arrangements, sale of bank assets to the plan, etc.

3. Related Bank Policies:

4. Related Issues:

FIDUCIARY COMPLIANCE RISK MANAGEMENT CHECKLIST

COMPLIANCE PROGRAM _____ Check, WP Ref.

or Initials

NUMBER _____ AS OF DATE _____

ERISA (SECTION 407)

1. Synoptic: This section provides an exception to the general prohibited transaction rules of Section 406 for the acquisition and holding of "qualifying" employer securities and real property. Essentially, it places a 10% limit in relation to total plan assets on the holding of such securities and real property in the aggregate. However, individual account plans in existence prior to September 2, 1974 that invested primarily in these assets, and defined benefit plans in existence as of the same date which specifically authorize the holding of a greater percentage are exempt from this limitation. Securities to qualify must meet a number of tests under this section, but they essentially cannot exceed 25% of the total market value of the issue and have to be marketable. For real estate to qualify, it must meet the following tests: a) must be a substantial number of parcels geographically dispersed, b) the parcels must be suitable for more than one use, c) the real property may be leased to one lessee (which may be the employer or an affiliate of the employer), and d) the acquisition and retention of such property has to comply with the diversification standards of Section 404 and all other requirements of Section 406.

2. Policy(ies)/Procedure(s): Should address monitoring of any holdings of employer securities or real property where the bank is a fiduciary to the plan to determine that such property is eligible for the Section

407 exception to the general prohibited transaction
rules of Section 406.

3. Related Bank Policies:

4. Related Issues:

FIDUCIARY COMPLIANCE RISK MANAGEMENT CHECKLIST

COMPLIANCE PROGRAM_____   Check, WP Ref.

or Initials

NUMBER _____ AS OF DATE _____

ERISA (SECTION 408)

1. Synoptic: This section provides statutory exemptions from the general prohibited transaction Section 406 for the following transaction types: a) loans to plan participants where the loans are made available to all participants on a reasonably equivalent basis, where loans are made under specific plan provisions, or where loans bear a reasonable rate of interest and are adequately secured; b) reasonable arrangements with a party in interest for office space, legal, accounting or other services necessary for plan operation assuming reasonable compensation; c) ESOP loans primarily for participant's benefits and with a reasonable interest rate; d) deposits in banks if the bank is a fiduciary of such plan; e) insurance contracts if the insurer is the employer or a party in interest owned by the employer; f) transactions between a plan and a collective investment fund maintained by a party in interest which is a bank; g) the making by a plan fiduciary of a distribution of the assets of the plan under Section 4044 of ERISA; and h) other transactions under Section 408(b)(1)-(13).

2. Policy(ies)/Procedure(s): Should address plan loans to participants and ESOP loans, specifically relating to reasonable rates of interest, collateral, and ensuring that the plan provides for such loans to participants.

3. Related Bank Policies:

4. Related Issues:

FIDUCIARY COMPLIANCE RISK MANAGEMENT CHECKLIST

COMPLIANCE PROGRAM _____ Check, WP Ref.

or Initials

NUMBER _____ AS OF DATE _____

INTERNAL REVENUE CODE CHAPTER 43
(EXCISE AND PENALTY TAXES)

1. Synoptic: This section of the Internal Revenue Code imposes taxes on a number of transactions, omissions, or other activities associated with employee benefit plans, including the following: a) Section 4971 re: tax for failure to meet minimum funding standard; b) Section 4972 re: tax on nondeductible contributions to qualified employer plans; c) Section 4973 re: tax on excess contributions to IRAs and Section 403(b) annuities; d) Section 4974 re: tax on excess accumulations in IRAs; e) Section 4975 re: 5% (or 100% if not corrected promptly) tax on prohibited transactions; f) Section 4976 re: 100% tax on disqualified welfare benefit; g) Section 4978 re: tax on certain ESOP distributions and allocations; h) Section 4979 re: tax on certain excess contributions; i) Section 4979A re: 50% tax on a prohibited allocation of securities by an ESOP; and j) Section 4981A re: tax on excess distributions.

2. Policy(ies)/Procedure(s): Should address those areas of responsibility that the bank, as a plan fiduciary, has to ensure that an excise or penalty tax is not imposed within these sections. For example, if the bank is trustee over an IRA, an excess accumulation tax may be imposed for which the bank is responsible if no notices of required distributions have been sent. Likewise, the bank may be responsible for an excess distribution tax if the bank is the party responsible for distributions under the plan

and distributes beyond the maximum allowable distribution under the plan.

3. Related Bank Policies:

4. Related Issues:

26CFR54.4975-7 re: statutory exemption from prohibited transaction provisions of Section 4975 for a loan to an ESOP which meets the exemption requirements of Section 4975(d)(3); 29CFR2550.408b-1 re: statutory exemption from prohibited transaction provisions of Section 4975 for a participant loan which meets the exemption requirements of Section 4975(d)(1).

FIDUCIARY COMPLIANCE RISK MANAGEMENT CHECKLIST

COMPLIANCE PROGRAM _____   Check, WP Ref.

or Initials

NUMBER _____ AS OF DATE _____

ESOP LOAN EXEMPTION—26CFR54.4975-7

1. Synoptic: This regulation, promulgated under IRC Section 4975(d)(3), sets standards to prevent selfdealing between the ESOP plan and the employer, its directors, officers, or any other parties in interest to the plan. The relevance to the bank as fiduciary is that any fiduciary should exercise cautious discretion in approving such loans and should be prepared to demonstrate that: a) the loan is in the best interests of the beneficiaries rather than, for example, selling shareholders (perhaps directors or officers of the company); b) the use of the loan proceeds is to: i) acquire qualifying employer securities, ii) repay the loan, or iii) repay a prior exempt loan; c) the exempt loan to the ESOP is without recourse to the ESOP; d) the rate of interest is reasonable; e) any loan default must limit the plan assets to be transferred to only satisfaction of the default; f) plan assets are released from encumbrance against the loan under stipulated IRS rules; g) an appropriate right of first refusal and put option is exercisable by plan participants for their best interests under well-defined IRS rules.

2. Policy(ies)/Procedure(s): Should address specific loan provisions to an ESOP for any account in which the bank is a fiduciary. In such cases, the bank has the risk of being responsible for prohibited transaction penalties and potential plan disqualification if all of the regulations pertaining to ESOP loans are not complied with.

3. Related Bank Policies:

4. Related Issues:

   IRC Section 401 re: Qualification for ESOPs; and 26CFR54.4975-11 re: ESOP requirements.

FIDUCIARY COMPLIANCE RISK MANAGEMENT CHECKLIST

COMPLIANCE PROGRAM _____ Check, WP Ref.

or Initials

NUMBER _____ AS OF DATE _____

PARTICIPANT LOAN EXEMPTION—29CFR2550.408b-1

1. Synoptic: This regulation, promulgated under IRC Section 4975(d)(1), exempts participant loans from the general prohibited transaction rules of ERISA Section 406 and IRC Section 4975 if the following five criteria are met: a) loans are available to all participants and beneficiaries on a reasonably equivalent basis; b) they are not made available to highly compensated employees in amounts greater than the amounts made available to other employees; c) they are made in accordance with specific provisions set forth in the plan; d) they bear a reasonable rate of interest; and e) they are adequately secured. Reasonable rates of interest must be market rates, based on the facts and circumstances surrounding the loan. Adequate security for the loan also places a cap of 50% of the participant's vested accrued benefit which can be used as collateral. The specific plan provisions must include: a) a procedure for determining a reasonable rate of interest, b) the type(s) of collateral that may secure a loan, c) the events that will constitute a loan default, and d) the steps that will be taken to preserve plan assets in the event of a default.

2. Policy(ies)/Procedure(s): Should specifically address the bank's responsibility for administering the loan programs of qualified plans, including its responsibility for disbursing funds only after verifying compliance with this regulation, its collection re-

sponsibilities, and other activities which could create a prohibited transaction and associated taxes.

3. Related Bank Policies:

4. Related Issues:

IRC Section 401 re: qualification and IRC Section 414 re: highly compensated employees; and Retirement Equity Act (REA) of 1984 re: spousal consent requirements for participant loans which could create risk to a fiduciary who extends the loan without seeking spousal consent.

FIDUCIARY COMPLIANCE RISK MANAGEMENT CHECKLIST

COMPLIANCE PROGRAM _____ Check, WP Ref.

or Initials

NUMBER _____ AS OF DATE _____

INTERNAL REVENUE CODE SECTION 401— QUALIFICATION

1. Synoptic: This section provides qualification requirements for benefit plans. It limits contribution
   amounts and distribution amounts, defines minimum
   vesting schedules, minimum participation requirements, prohibits discriminating in favor of highly
   compensated employees, specifies requirements for
   written plans and plan permanency, and provides
   other protections to participants prior to allowing the
   plan to be qualified for tax advantaged treatment.
   Banks that provide master or prototype plans often
   perform the various tests or are responsible for ensuring that some or all of the qualification requirements are met, e.g., vesting schedules meet the
   required minimums, participation meets the minimum standards, etc. Also, plans qualified under IRC
   Section 401 are eligible, under Revenue Ruling 81-
   100, to be collectively invested in a commingled tax
   exempt fund.

2. Policy(ies)/Procedure(s): Should address the required responsibilities the bank has for any accounts to ensure qualification requirements are met
   and that the plan meets the qualification requirements. Master or prototype plans sponsored by the
   bank should be updated under a specific set of policies and procedures, including IRS Determination
   Letters to assure plan qualification.

3. Related Bank Policies:

4. Related Issues:

Other IRC Sections, e.g., 414 re: highly compensated employees, 415 re: benefit and contribution
limits, 416 re: top heavy plans, 401(k) re: ADP testing of cash or deferred arrangements, 403(b) re:
annuity plans, 457 re: government plans, 408 re:
IRAs.

FIDUCIARY COMPLIANCE RISK MANAGEMENT CHECKLIST

COMPLIANCE PROGRAM_____   Check, WP Ref.

or Initials

NUMBER_____ AS OF DATE_____

REGULATION Z—PLAN LOANS

1. Synoptic: Section 226.2 of this regulation defines coverage under this regulation to anyone who extends consumer credit more than 25 times (or 5 times for loans secured by a dwelling) in a calendar year. This number must be applied one "look-back" year as well as the current year. For trusts, each individual trust is considered a creditor; therefore, Regulation Z is applicable only at individual trust levels where the trust made more than 25 consumer loans (or 5 for mortgages) either in the current or preceding year. Subject to Regulation Z, the necessary Truth In Lending Disclosures must be met to satisfy the regulation.

2. Policy(ies)/Procedure(s): Should address the monitoring of each trust account, primarily employee benefit trusts with loan provisions, for the applicability of Regulation Z Truth In Lending Disclosures and have appropriate follow-up standards.

3. Related Bank Policies:

4. Related Issues:

CORPORATE BOND TRUSTEE AND AGENCY SERVICES

This very complex fiduciary business area primarily provides indenture trusteeships on bond issues as well as transfer, paying and exchange and tender agency functions for corporations, municipalities, and other entities.

As corporate trustee, the bank has a fiduciary responsibility to the bondholders of a debt issue. The fiduciary duties include: a) collection of funds from the obligor for the payment of principal and interest to the bondholders, b) maintenance of the accounting records to determine funds have been received, c) the investment of funds (which may be directed by the terms of the bond indenture), d) the receipt and review of documents, e) disbursement of funds to the bondholders for principal and interest payments, f) monitoring actions taken by the issuer or obligor to ensure compliance with the governing document, and g) ensuring that the obligor is financially sound to meet its principal and interest obligations. Should a default occur, the trustee's duties become very serious in relation to the protection of bondholders. The trustee must act in accordance with the "Prudent Man Standard" in the enforcement of a bondholder's rights under the Trust Indenture Reform Act of 1990.

The capacities of registrar/transfer agent and paying agent are more ministerial in scope and are essentially agency relationships with the issuer of the securities. When acting as registrar/transfer agent, the trustee affects the transfer of securities and maintains records of ownership.

The paying agent role is limited to paying principal, premium, and interest on securities. Other agency roles include: tender agent, the acceptance of securities from holders exercising their option to "put" holdings back to the issuer, and conversion agent which is the receipt of securities for conversion into the stock of the issuer.

Operational functions include the issuance and registration or transfer of securities, maintenance of bondholder records, reconciling the funding received from the obligor to bondholder payments, and the processing of principal, premium, and interest payments.

The INHERENT RISK in offering corporate trustee and agency products and services has several factors. The competitive nature of this business, in most markets, often creates thin profit margins. As this book is being published, interest rates are at their lowest levels in 20 years. Historically, this means a flood of financing or refinancing vehicles would be brought to market. However, because the economy is in a recession, many businesses are deferring borrowing and many economists project interest rates will continue to decline. The recessionary nature of today's economy can also increase payment default levels. For bonds secured by mortgages, it can cause the underlying collateral to be insufficient if the mortgage payments are in default. The state of the market and the economy, clearly, significantly affect the volume of business in these products. Therefore, MARKET and ECONOMIC RISK are large parts of the INHERENT RISK EQUATION.

Other INHERENT RISK factors include: 1) THE COMPLEXITY OF THE ACCOUNTING SYSTEMS that have to be designed to track the securities holdings, interest or dividend payments, transfer agency activities, tax impact, inventory control over unissued securities, etc., as well as the administrative information contained in the indenture and ancillary authoritative documents; 2) THE CAPABILITIES OF THE STAFF, which creates the need for extensive training in corporate trust administration and operations; and 3) THE MAGNITUDE OF LEGAL AND REGULATORY SANCTIONS involved in this business line, including: the legal aspects of the indenture, the IRS regulations pertaining to income tax reporting to bondholders and arbitrage concerns associated with municipal bond offerings, and the level of federal laws including the Trust Indenture Reform Act of 1990 and SEC Regulations around transfer agency regulations.

These risks, as with any risks, create costs—costs of compliance, costs to train people appropriately, costs to build suitable accounting systems, etc.

DECISION TO ACCEPT NEW APPOINTMENT

Residual risks associated with the management decision of accepting a new corporate trustee or agency appointment are as follows:

- Obligor may not be financially solid, or issue may cause high leverage or other speculative aspect for the issue and may impair repayment ability.

- Potential for costly legal expenses on issues where the trustee must use legal counsel to protect bondholders.

- Potential for environmental problems if bond issue is secured by real property.

- Potential for conflicts of interest (both statutory under the Trust Indenture Reform Act disqualifying conflict provisions or other conflict situations).

- Possibility for duties to exceed capabilities of trustee.

- If successor appointment, prior trustee actions may have created problems which successor will inherit.

- Possibility that agents selected are not capable.

- Legal complexities, including tax laws (e.g., arbitrage issues) may cause problems.

- Responsibilities may be described vaguely causing duties to "fall between the cracks."

- Profit margin is insufficient for duties, responsibilities, and liabilities.

- Bond issue may be politically or socially sensitive, causing embarrassment or negative goodwill for the bank.

- Financial set up, purpose, or general economic benefit of bond issue may be questionable.

Controls to mitigate the residual risk in accepting new corporate trust or agency appointments include the following:

- Financial and credit analysis performed on obligor.

- Account acceptance standards which assure proper due diligence is performed over acceptance of: a) speculative or highly leveraged bond issues, b) issues which could put the bank in the middle of sensitive political or social concerns, and c) issues secured by real property which may be environmentally unsound.

- Proper legal review over the indenture to ensure all duties are clearly delineated and that tax issues (primarily for tax exempt bond issues) have been properly scrutinized to ensure the trustee does not cause the issue to become taxable.

- Cost analysis to assure the appointment meets the bank's required margin.

- Policies and procedures requiring review of authorized signatures to release disbursements.

- Policies and procedures for the initial account setup requiring minimum levels of required information and a checklist for opening accounts and committee approval.

ADMINISTRATION ACTIVITIES

Residual risks associated with the administration of corporate trust and agency accounts include the following: (Note: we have also included those risks which would be created within the operating support area of corporate trust administration since corporate trust operations is very different from other areas of trust operations which support managed and custodial assets of accounts, but are not responsible for a second tier of individuals, in this case the bondholders.)

- Noncompliance with the indenture covenants and/or the Trust Indenture Reform Act of 1990.

- Improper handling of bond redemptions, put, and call activity in accordance with the indenture and industry standards.

- Improper or untimely disbursement of funds to bondholders for interest (or dividends if the bank is a dividend paying agent), redemptions, exchanges, bond calls, etc.

- Excessive expense to the bank to protect bondholders in the event of a default by the obligor, including litigation expenses.

- Improper file maintenance and/or poor custody practices over collateral or credit enhancement files, such as not properly recording mortgages, U.C.C. filings, inadequate or expired insurance, or letters of credit which could adversely affect a bondholder's interest and cause loss to the holders.

- Failure to perform the necessary secondary market disclosures for bond issues.

- Inadequate procedures for tax filings, including compliance with the Tax Equity and Fiscal Responsibility Act of 1982 (TEFRA) requirements for bondholder payments.

- Acting on instructions that are not authorized or are contrary to the terms of the indenture.

- Losses due to the duplicate payment of interest, dividends, proceeds from redemption or calls.

- Losses from theft, misplacement, or disappearance of bearer instruments.

- Losses from payment of bond proceeds over a stop payment.

- Losses from payment of bond proceeds from a bond which has not been physically marked as canceled or paid.

- Losses resulting from co-paying agent activities, e.g., loss of bearer bonds or negotiable coupons.

- Losses due to having to reimburse bondholders because of insufficient notification of bond calls.

- Losses from overpaying co-paying agents or not collecting enough from the obligor or co-paying agents for bondholder principal or income payments.

- Losses from theft or embezzlement of bearer bond inventory or unissued registered bonds.

- Losses from improper trade settlement or turnaround errors causing bondholder loss or improper payment of dividends on stock issues, e.g., by not considering "ex-dividend" date properly.

■ Curtailment of business activities (if acting as a registered transfer agent) due to inability to comply with the turn-around requirements of the SEC.

■ Losses from payment for a security which has been duly reported as missing with the Securities Information Center (SIC) or loss from not reporting a missing security with the SIC after proper notification from the security holder.

■ Losses from failure to comply with the records retention requirements or the requirements for reporting "aged record differences" for registered transfer agents.

■ Losses from improper or untimely reporting of tax information, e.g., 1099 reporting and certification of Taxpayer ID numbers under TEFRA with Form W-9.

■ Losses from statutory penalties associated with violating local abandoned property (escheat) statutes.

■ Losses due to inaccurate interpretation of who has the authority to direct investments under the indenture.

■ Losses due to vagueness of the indenture in specifying what authorized investments the trustee can make at its discretion.

■ Losses from violating the IRS regulations concerning arbitrage restrictions on investments involving tax exempt securities, thereby potentially converting the bond issue to a taxable issue and causing loss to the bondholders.

■ Losses from litigation and legal expenses due to a disqualifying conflict event taking place, such as the issue going into default while the trustee is also a lender to the obligor.

Controls to mitigate residual risk in corporate trust and agency administration activities include the following:

- Procedures to ensure an accurate and concise synoptic record of the indenture provisions for day-to-day administration of the account.

- Ticklers and checklists to monitor interest dates, potential call dates, dates for required funding from the obligor for interest payments, sinking fund payments, calls, and partial calls, etc.

- Procedures that identify any potential conflict of interest situation which could become a disqualifying conflict of interest if the bond issue goes into default.

- Policies and procedures which require that all instructions given by the obligor or other authorized party be in writing.

- Physical controls over bearer bonds, coupons, and unissued bond inventory to prevent theft.

- Reconciliation controls to ensure that the account is properly funded at all times, including reconciliations with co-paying agent's accounts.

- Proper recordkeeping and record retention procedures to ensure that the turnaround requirements of the SEC are met for registered transfer agents.

- Proper reconciliations of master issuer records against individual bondholder (or stockholder) records to ensure that all out of balance conditions are investigated and corrected in a timely manner so as to not have to report aged record differences to the regulators and to the issuing companies.

- Proper reconciliations of both debit and credit suspense accounts, as well as the resolution of outstanding differences to ensure against losses due to insufficient funds in the paying agent accounts and to ensure compliance with relevant escheat laws.

- Procedures to ensure that securities being redeemed have not been reported to the SIC as missing or stolen.

- Procedures to ensure prompt notification to the SIC of any securities reported by bondholders (stockholders) to the bank as missing or stolen.

- Procedures to reconcile 1099 interest or dividend reporting against bondholder interest payment ledgers to ensure properly reported amounts to the IRS.

FIDUCIARY COMPLIANCE RISK MANAGEMENT CHECKLIST

COMPLIANCE PROGRAM_____   Check, WP Ref.

or Initials

NUMBER_____ AS OF DATE_____

SECURITIES LAWS AND REGULATIONS
(17CFR240.17f-1)

1. Synoptic: This regulation deals with the reporting and inquiry on missing, counterfeit, or stolen securities. It requires registered transfer agents to register with the Securities Information Center. For missing or lost securities, it generally requires reporting within two business days of the discovery of the missing security; if the discovery is the result of an asset verification procedure, reporting must be done within ten business days after the count is completed. Counterfeit securities are to be reported within one business day after their discovery as counterfeit. Reports are to be made on Form X-17F-1A. The reports as well as confirmations on inquiries from the SIC must be kept in readily accessible form for three years to indemnify the bank against loss.

2. Policy(ies)/ Procedure(s): Should address the timely registration with the SIC, the timely reporting of securities which are missing, lost, or counterfeit, and the timely inquiry regarding securities coming into the bank's possession. The U.S. government, agencies, bond coupons, securities without CUSIP numbers, and certain other securities are exempt from reporting.

3. Related Bank Policies:

4. Related Issues:

FIDUCIARY COMPLIANCE RISK MANAGEMENT CHECKLIST

COMPLIANCE PROGRAM_____   Check, WP Ref.

or Initials

NUMBER_____ AS OF DATE_____

SECURITIES LAWS AND REGULATIONS
(17CFR240.17f-2)

1. Synoptic: This regulation deals with the fingerprint-
    ing of securities personnel and requires that regis-
    tered transfer agents' partners, directors, officers,
    and employees be fingerprinted and that the finger-
    prints be submitted to the U.S. Attorney General for
    appropriate processing. The parties above, to be in-
    cludible, must have access to securities, monies, or
    original books relating to such securities or monies
    or have supervisory responsibilities over such par-
    ties. Fingerprinting must be attempted at least three
    times before an exemption is granted for the illeg-
    ible prints of the individual.

2. Policy(ies)/Procedure(s): Should address the finger-
    printing requirements and specific identification of
    those individuals who must be fingerprinted, as well
    as the reporting requirements. There are also spe-
    cific record retention requirements of the regulation
    which must be complied with under sections (d)(1)
    and (d)(2).

3. Related Bank Policies:

4. Related Issues:

FIDUCIARY COMPLIANCE RISK MANAGEMENT CHECKLIST

COMPLIANCE PROGRAM_____   Check, WP Ref.

or Initials

NUMBER _____ AS OF DATE _____

SECURITIES LAWS AND REGULATIONS
(17CFR240.17Ad1-14)

1. Synoptic: This set of rules governs registered transfer agent activities and specifically covers the following: Ad-1: Definitions; Ad-2: Turnaround,
   processing, and forwarding of items; Ad-3: Limitations on expansion; Ad-4: Applicability of various
   paragraphs; Ad-5: Written inquiries and requests;
   Ad-6: Recordkeeping; Ad-7: Record retention; Ad-8:
   Securities position listings; Ad-9: Definitions for Ad-
   10-14; Ad-10: Prompt posting of certificate detail to
   master files, maintenance of accurate records, and
   communications with issuers on problems; Ad-11:
   Reports to issuers and regulators on aged record
   differences in the reconciliations between detail and
   master files; Ad-12: Safeguarding of securities and
   funds; Ad-13: Annual study and evaluation of internal accounting control; and Ad-14: Tender agent requirements.

2. Policy(ies)/Procedure(s): Should address specific
   requirements of all pertinent paragraphs; detailed
   paragraph analysis should be incorporated in database within this category.

3. Related Bank Policies:

4. Related Issues:

FIDUCIARY COMPLIANCE RISK MANAGEMENT CHECKLIST

COMPLIANCE PROGRAM _____   Check, WP Ref.

or Initials

NUMBER _____ AS OF DATE _____

SECURITIES LAWS AND REGULATIONS (17CFR240.17Ad2)

1. Synoptic: This paragraph requires that for registered transfer agents, the turnaround (for transfer agent functions) and processing (for registrar functions) of at least 90% of "routine" items be done within three business days and one business day, respectively. For an "exempt transfer agent," the turnaround requirement is five business days. This section also requires a report be filed with the appropriate bank regulator and the SEC within ten business days after the end of any month where these turnaround or processing requirements are not met.

2. Policy(ies)/Procedure(s): Should address the mechanics of monitoring the turnaround requirements and determining routine items versus nonroutine items as well as the calculation requirements necessary to ensure compliance.

3. Related Bank Policies:

4. Related Issues:

17CFR240.17Ad1 re: definitions of "routine items," "turnaround," "processing" and "cut-off time"; 17CFR240.17Ad4 re: definition of "exempt transfer agent"; 17CFR240.17Ad3 re: curtailment of transfer agent activities if turnaround and processing requirements are not met; 17CFR240.17Ad6 re: log of information necessary to substantiate turnaround and processing compliance; 17CFR240.17Ad12 re: safeguarding of securities in the performance of transfer agent activities; and 17CFR240.17Ad7 re: record retention.

FIDUCIARY COMPLIANCE RISK MANAGEMENT CHECKLIST

COMPLIANCE PROGRAM_____   Check, WP Ref.

or Initials

NUMBER _____ AS OF DATE _____

SECURITIES LAWS AND REGULATIONS
(17CFR240.17Ad5)

1. Synoptic: This paragraph discusses requirements of the transfer agent to respond to written inquiries and requests for information regarding the status of items presented for transfer. The following are the requirements: a) for anyone requesting information regarding the status of an item presented within the last 6 months, the agent must respond within 5 business days; b) for any broker/dealer requesting whether the transfer agent has possession of an item presented at any time, the agent must respond within 5 business days; c) for anyone (other than broker/dealers) requesting whether the transfer agent has possession of an item presented within the last 30 days, the agent must respond within 10 business days; d) for anyone requesting transcript activity of an item presented within the last 6 months, the agent must provide (and can charge a service fee) within 20 business days; and e) for any other relevant requests for information and inquiries, the agent must respond promptly.

2. Policy(ies)/Procedure(s): Should address the monitoring of such inquiries and requests for transfer agent items, including the records needed to demonstrate compliance with this paragraph.

3. Related Bank Policies:

---

4. Related Issues:

17CFR240.17Ad6 re: log of records needed to demonstrate compliance; 17CFR240.17Ad7 re: record retention requirements; 17CFR240.17Ad1 re: definitions.

FIDUCIARY COMPLIANCE RISK MANAGEMENT CHECKLIST

COMPLIANCE PROGRAM _____   Check, WP Ref.

or Initials

NUMBER _____ AS OF DATE _____

SECURITIES LAWS AND REGULATIONS
(17CFR240.17Ad10-11)

1. Synoptic: These two paragraphs discuss the mini-
    mum standards for the prompt and accurate crea-
    tion and maintenance of issuer and holder records
    and the reporting of serious difficulties in the per-
    formance of transfer agent activities to the issuer(s)
    of the securities and to the appropriate bank regula-
    tor. Specifically, the posting of the certificate detail
    to properly reflect the registered owners of the se-
    curities and the reconciliation of all holders to the
    issuer master record must be done promptly and
    accurately. Differences must be aged and aged re-
    cord differences greater than the amounts outlined
    in Ad11 must be reported to issuers and the regula-
    tors. Such required reporting could jeopardize the
    relationship the bank has with the issuing compa-
    nies; therefore, it is critical that the bank post the
    certificate detail promptly and reconcile promptly to
    avoid having to prepare the required reports of
    Ad11.

2. Policy(ies)/Procedure(s): Should address the re-
    quirements of prompt posting of certificate detail
    and the reconciliations between the detail list of se-
    curities holders to the master control record by is-
    sue, including identification of any discrepancies
    and proper management follow-up to prevent hav-
    ing to report difficulties as required in paragraph
    Ad11.

3. Related Bank Policies:

4. Related Issues:

17CFR240.17Ad8 re: definitions of "certificate de-tail," "master security-holder file," "subsidiary file," "record difference," and various parties.

FIDUCIARY COMPLIANCE RISK MANAGEMENT CHECKLIST

COMPLIANCE PROGRAM _____   Check, WP Ref.

or Initials

NUMBER _____ AS OF DATE _____

SECURITIES LAWS AND REGULATIONS
(17CFR240.17Ad13)

1. Synoptic: This paragraph requires an annual study and evaluation of the internal accounting control of registered transfer agents. The report has to be prepared by an independent accountant concerning the system of internal accounting control and related procedures for the transfer of record ownership and the safeguarding of related securities and funds. The report must be filed within 90 calendar days of the date of such study and evaluation. This paragraph also details the minimum scope of such study and evaluation and its required objectives. Also, there is a special provision for the bank allowing the study to be prepared for the bank's board of directors, or its audit committee, instead of being filed with the SEC as long as the requirements of Ad13 are met.

2. Policy(ies)/Procedure(s): Should address the performance of such study and evaluation, including the selection of the independent accountants, monitoring of the scope to ensure compliance with this paragraph, and corrective action as required under this paragraph to material findings.

3. Related Bank Policies:

4. Related Issues:

Requires review of compliance with Ad2, Ad10, and Ad12, as well as other requirements of scope.

3. Related Bank Policies:

4. Related Issues:

   Requires review of compliance with Ad2, Ad10, and Ad12, as well as other requirements of scope.

FIDUCIARY COMPLIANCE RISK MANAGEMENT CHECKLIST

COMPLIANCE PROGRAM_____   Check, WP Ref.

or Initials

NUMBER _____ AS OF DATE _____

SECURITIES LAWS AND REGULATIONS
(BOND TRUSTEESHIPS)

1. Synoptic: The Trust Indenture Act (TIA) of 1939, amended by the Trust Indenture Reform Act (TIRA) of 1990, govern most corporate bond issues above $10 million except those exempt from the provisions of the Securities Act of 1933 under paragraphs (2)-(8) and (11) of subsection 3(a) of that act. TIRA requires, where applicable, that an eligible trustee (defined in Section 310) protect the rights and best interests of bondholders (for the purposes outlined in Section 302) by performing certain duties and taking on certain responsibilities (under Section 315). Section 313 imposes requirements on the trustee to report on its continued eligibility as trustee to the bondholders as well as other reporting requirements. Section 314 imposes an obligation on the obligor of the issue to demonstrate compliance with the trust indenture at inception and annually thereafter. Section 310 also provides for disqualification of the indenture trustee under certain conditions.

2. Policy(ies)/Procedure(s): Should address, on an issue-by-issue basis, during the account acceptance process, whether the issue is subject to TIRA, if so, and set in motion monitoring and compliance efforts with the relevant sections of the act.

3. Related Bank Policies:

4. Related Issues:

Detailed sections on TIRA compliance issues.

FIDUCIARY COMPLIANCE RISK MANAGEMENT CHECKLIST

COMPLIANCE PROGRAM_____   Check, WP Ref.

or Initials

NUMBER _____ AS OF DATE _____

SECURITIES LAWS AND REGULATIONS
(TIRA—SECTION 310)

1. Synoptic: Section 310 prescribes the rules for eligibility and disqualification of the trustee. There are ten situations under which the trustee is disqualified if the bond issue goes into default. (Under the 1939 TIA, the trustee was disqualified even if the bond issue was not in default.) The ten situations are as follows: 1) if the trustee is also a trustee under a different subordinated issue of the same obligor; 2) if the trustee, its directors, or executive officers are an underwriter of the issue; 3) if the trustee is affiliated with the obligor or underwriter; 4) if the trustee, its directors, or executive officers are a director, executive officer, or principal of the obligor or underwriter; 5) if 10% of the voting securities of the trustee is owned by the obligor or underwriter; 6) if 10% of the securities of the obligor or underwriter is owned by the trustee; 7) if 5% of any affiliate of the obligor is owned by the trustee; 8) if the trustee owns 10% of any class of securities of anyone owning 50% of the voting shares of the obligor; 9) if the trustee holds for others 25% of any class of securities that would cause disqualification under (6)-(8) above; and 10) if the trustee is also a creditor of the obligor. (NOTE: there are some additional calculations required in some of these percentage holding provisions, but the essence of the disqualifying holding is as stated.)

2. Policy(ies)/Procedure(s): Should address the situations that could cause disqualification if the bond issue goes into default, as the trustee has significant duties to the bondholders upon a default.

3. Related Bank Policies:

4. Related Issues:

   Section 313 reporting on continued eligibility.

FIDUCIARY COMPLIANCE RISK MANAGEMENT CHECKLIST

COMPLIANCE PROGRAM _____   Check, WP Ref.

or Initials

NUMBER _____ AS OF DATE _____

SECURITIES LAWS AND REGULATIONS
(TIRA—SECTION 313)

1. Synoptic: Under TIA of 1939, the trustee was required to report annually, each May, as to the following: a) the trustee's continued eligibility to act; b) the nature and amount of advances made to the obligor; c) any indebtedness by the obligor to the bank in the bank's individual capacity; d) property and funds in the trustee's possession from the obligor; e) any releases of collateral over the bond obligation; f) additional issuances of securities by the obligor; and g) any trustee action which materially affects the bondholders. TIRA of 1990 amends this so that the trustee only needs to report to the extent a change has occurred in the previous 12 months. Note, however, that the bank would be required to perform the 25% test each May 15 of holdings of the bond issue in fiduciary accounts for which the bank is the beneficial owner (or has discretion and power to vote, as applicable).

2. Policy(ies)/Procedure(s): Should address the requirement of reporting to bondholders at inception and where there has been a change in those items required under Section 313 as well as proper monitoring of the reports being sent.

3. Related Bank Policies:

4. Related Issues:

Section 314 requirements that the obligor certify to the trustee that the indenture provisions are being complied with; any noncompliance issues must be reported by the trustee under Section 313. Also, Section 315 requirements of notifications to the bondholders of default.

FIDUCIARY COMPLIANCE RISK MANAGEMENT CHECKLIST

COMPLIANCE PROGRAM _____   Check, WP Ref.

or Initials

NUMBER _____ AS OF DATE _____

SECURITIES LAWS AND REGULATIONS (STOCK EXCHANGE RULES)

1. Synoptic: There are two exchange rules for transfer agents: a) NYSE Rule 496 requirements for independent agents acting as, or in lieu of, New York City transfer agents of securities listed on the NYSE; and b) ASE Rule 891 requirements in order to qualify as a transfer agent for securities listed on the American Stock Exchange (where the company is not acting as its own transfer agent) for i) transfer agents located in New York City and ii) transfer agents located out of New York City where there is no transfer agent in New York City for the stock. Both rules require the following: a) offices in Manhattan satisfactory to the respective exchanges; b) a 48-hour turnaround between receipt and pickup; c) the transfer agent assumes total responsibility and liability for securities from deposit to redelivery at the window; d) sufficient experience of personnel; and e) securities received before the close of business on any day that create a "securities holder right" issue (e.g., record date) to record the receipt as of that date. Rule 496 requires transfer agent capital of $10 million. Rule 891 requires capital of $3 million. Rule 496 requires insurance coverage of $25 million; Rule 891 requires insurance of $10 million. The agent or drop location under both rules must be located south of Chambers Street.

2. Policy(ies)/Procedure(s): Should address requirements of both rules to ensure compliance with
   Stock Exchange requirements.

3. Related Bank Policies:

4. Related Issues:

   Contained herein

INVESTMENT PORTFOLIO MANAGEMENT/COLLECTIVE INVESTMENT FUNDS

Trust departments can offer their client base various portfolio management services. Most investment management units are responsible for supporting trust investment related activities. Discretionary portfolio management services can include the management of pooled or commingled funds (for bona fide trust accounts and employee benefit plans) as well as separately managed accounts for all trust product lines. Additionally, these units can support the discretionary investment activities of the trust entity and provide security trading services and settlement for customer directed transactions.

The portfolio management area is sometimes broken into two divisions. One division is responsible for investment research re-

93

sulting in investment decisions over particular issues based on the investment strategy and theory employed by the department. The result of these decisions is a list of fiduciary quality investments and is commonly referred to as the "approved list" of equity, debt, and other securities. The other division is responsible for the portfolio management of collective investment funds and/or individual account portfolio management. The investment person for individually managed accounts works as a team with the administrative account officer to ensure that suitable fiduciary quality investments are used within a trust portfolio.

INHERENT RISKS in the portfolio management product obviously include not making good investment decisions and having a poor track record in the collective investment funds. This situation could create a competitive disadvantage for the bank in attracting new customers (particularly new employee benefit plans which are keenly aware of the need for solid investment performance). Therefore, staffing this area with competent investment researchers and portfolio managers is extremely important as well as developing portfolio modeling tools and having up to date access to financial markets and industry and company financial analysis.

Also included in the INHERENT RISK factors are the economy and related reactions in the financial markets. Downturns in the economy not only can bring negative investment results, but can also cut into fees since market values of the assets are normally large factors in the computation of fees.

DECISION TO ACCEPT NEW APPOINTMENT

Residual risks associated with the management decision to accept a new investment management account or to provide collective investment funds managed by the bank include the following:

- Vagueness in the language of the investment management contract which may cause investments to be made which do not meet the objectives of the principal.

- Volume of trades for the account may be beyond the capabilities of the investment area or may create operational problems for the trade settlement area.

- If the portfolio management is part of a trust relationship, there may be unsuitable assets in the trust that the portfolio manager recommends to be liquidated. The customer or administrative officer, however, may be reluctant to do so, thereby creating potential loss to the account.

- For collective investment funds, the portfolio manager must only invest in assets consistent with the fund's objectives.

- For ERISA accounts, the portfolio management area may have responsibility for assets in plans where there is no registered investment advisor, but has not been informed by the administrative officer of this situation.

- Although all of the assets on the approved list are fiduciary quality, there may be assets in discretionary accounts that are not fiduciary quality or that have not been reviewed on an annual basis because the portfolio management area has not recommended these assets or has recommended their liquidation.

Controls to mitigate residual risk in accepting new portfolio management accounts or using the portfolio management area in existing account relationships include the following:

- Procedures should exist which ensure that the investment management contracts are consistent with the portfolio manager's ability to properly manage the portfolio, including discussion of outside advice, directions from the principal, etc.

- Procedures should exist to allow the portfolio to properly divest the account of holdings of investments that are not on the approved list or do not meet the stated objectives of the account.

■   Procedures should exist to approve the appointment of
     the bank as portfolio manager.

ADMINISTRATION ACTIVITIES

Residual risks associated with the administration of portfolio management accounts or collective investment funds include the following:

■   Misunderstanding or lack of knowledge of a change in
     the investment objectives for the account.

■   Poor execution of trades causing purchase prices to be ex-
     cessive or sales prices to be too low.

■   Purchase of investments without adequate funds in the
     account to settle the trade, thereby creating an overdraft
     in the account.

■   Investment directions being given by the principal or an-
     other outside advisor which are not recognized by the
     trade settlement area on settlement date, thereby causing
     the transaction to fail and a loss to the account.

■   Investing a nonqualified account, e.g., agency account in
     a collective investment fund, thereby violating provisions
     of 12CFR9.18.

■   Investing common trust funds of more than 10% in one
     single issue, thereby violating the concentration limits of
     12CFR9.18.

■   Overselling a security or selling a security that is not
     owned by the account, thereby creating a loss to the ac-
     count.

■   Investing in assets where the bank has a potential or real
     conflict of interest.

- Using material inside information to purchase or sell a security and violating Rule 10b-5.

- Violating securities laws, such as Rule 144, by selling control or restricted stock without satisfying the required holding period, volume limitations, and disclosure requirements.

Controls to mitigate residual risk in administration activities for portfolio management accounts include the following:

- Policies and procedures requiring that all outside directions be given in writing and will be accepted only if they do not conflict with the terms of the contract.

- Policies and procedures should exist requiring all assets to be reviewed at least annually and any assets that are not fiduciary quality to be liquidated for discretionary accounts. Further, the policy should require that any deviations to the policy must be approved by executive management within the trust area.

- Policies and procedures should exist to assure compliance with 12CFR9.18 regarding collective investment funds.

- Policies and procedures should be in place to prevent against any trading on material inside information.

- Policies and procedures should be in place to prevent against any potential conflict situations, e.g., accepting financial benefits from a fund sponsor, investing fiduciary funds in 12b-1 mutual funds, investing in bonds underwritten by the bank, etc.

The following Fiduciary Compliance Risk Management Checklists include: collective investment fund, securities regulations, and conflict of interest compliance issues. We have included these under the portfolio management chapter since they all relate to assets in the account, even though the assets may not have been purchased by the portfolio management area. We believe that the portfolio management function is the best centralized area to monitor (or at least report upon) the compliance issues since it handles assets for the various products, i.e., personal trusts, employee benefit plans, as well as its own management agency accounts.

FIDUCIARY COMPLIANCE RISK MANAGEMENT CHECKLIST

COMPLIANCE PROGRAM_____   Check, WP Ref.

or Initials

NUMBER _____ AS OF DATE _____

SECURITIES TRADING ACTIVITIES (12CFR12.3)

1. Synoptic: This regulation, 12CFR12, was promulgated under 12USC92 and 12USC24 and deals
   with recordkeeping and confirmation requirements
   for securities transactions of national banks. FDIC
   regulation 344 is its counterpart. Paragraph 12.3 requires a three-year record retention over four types
   of records: 1) chronological trade record, 2) trade
   record by account, 3) order ticket record, and 4)
   broker record including commissions allocated and
   paid to each broker for the last three years.

2. Policy(ies)/Procedure(s): Should address the level
   of information required for each of the four record
   types, as required by the regulation, as well as ac-
   cessibility to the records when the trade ticket
   authorization process is automated.

3. Related Bank Policies:

4. Related Issues:

   a. Various Federal Reserve and SEC counterpart
      regulations

FIDUCIARY COMPLIANCE RISK MANAGEMENT CHECKLIST

COMPLIANCE PROGRAM _____   Check, WO Ref.

or Initials

NUMBER _____ AS OF DATE _____

SECURITIES TRADING ACTIVITIES (12CFR12.4)

1. Synoptic: 12.4 requires that the bank maintain, for three years, and mail to the customer, within five business days, a broker confirmation or the bank's written advice of all securities transactions (except as provided in 12.5) disclosing the following: 1) name of bank, 2) name of customer, 3) capacity of bank, 4) date of execution and statement that time of execution will be furnished upon notice, 5) amount of remuneration to brokers, 6) amount of remuneration received by bank, and 7) name of broker or person from whom security was bought or sold.

2. Policy(ies)/Procedure(s): Should address the form of notification requirements of 12.4 except as provided by 12.5.

3. Related Bank Policies:

4. Related Issues:

   a. Exceptions in 12.5

   b. FDIC Regulation 344

FIDUCIARY COMPLIANCE RISK MANAGEMENT CHECKLIST

COMPLIANCE PROGRAM _____   Check, WP Ref.

or Initials

NUMBER _____ AS OF DATE _____

SECURITIES TRADING ACTIVITIES (12CFR12.5)

1. Synoptic: 12.5 requires the notifications of 12.4 to be sent to the customer within five business days of the broker confirmation receipt by the bank or the following alternative notification methods: a) if directed agency account, as contracted in the agency letter of instructions, b) if discretionary account other than an agency account, upon written request of a valid powerholder, c) if a discretionary agency account, a customer statement showing all transactions relating to securities sent at least each three months to the customer will satisfy the notification requirements, or d) if a collective fund, 12CFR9.18(b)(5) will apply.

2. Policy(ies)/Procedure(s): Should address the preparation and mailing of notifications for those accounts required to receive five-day notification; and should provide a method to identify other accounts which use the other allowable alternative notification methods under 12.5.

3. Related Bank Policies:

4. Related Issues:
   a. FDIC 344
   b. Regulation 9.18(b)(5) for CIF trades

FIDUCIARY COMPLIANCE RISK MANAGEMENT CHECKLIST

COMPLIANCE PROGRAM _____   Check, WP Ref.

or Initials

NUMBER _____ AS OF DATE _____

SECURITIES TRADING ACTIVITIES (12CFR12.6)

1. Synoptic: 12.6 requires written policies and procedures which address the following: a) assignment of
   responsibilities for supervision of anyone who
   places orders or executes securities transactions; b)
   fair and equitable allocation of securities prices and
   commissions among accounts for block trades; c)
   fair and equitable allocation of prices in cross-or-
   ders; and d) the reporting, each calendar quarter,
   by anyone who has traded more than $10,000
   worth of securities during the quarter (excluding,
   U.S., U.S. agency and mutual funds) for their own
   account if that person had influence over, or knowledge of recommendations to purchase or sell securities for customers.

2. Policy(ies)/Procedure(s): Required by this section
   for those activities noted above; specifically, should
   require central authoritative, control point for the
   $10,000 report as well as a requirement that "null"
   reports be sent.

3. Related Bank Policies:

4. Related Issues:
   a. Ethics statements
   b. Insider trading rules

FIDUCIARY COMPLIANCE RISK MANAGEMENT CHECKLIST

COMPLIANCE PROGRAM _____   Check, WP Ref.

or Initials

NUMBER _____ AS OF DATE _____

SECURITIES TRADING ACTIVITIES
(TRUST BANKING CIRCULAR 25)

1. Synoptic: Trust Banking Circular (TBC) 25 discusses the use of commission payments by fiduciaries and makes reference to SEC Release
34-23170 on soft-dollar arrangements and DOL release 86-1 on fiduciary responsibility in soft-dollar
arrangements under ERISA. Essentially, it states
that: a) the investment manager must be able to
demonstrate a fair and equitable allocation of the
soft-dollar arrangement; b) the value of the research
in the arrangement is reasonable in relation to the
commissions paid; c) if the arrangement includes
both research and nonresearch services, the investment manager must clearly distinguish such difference; d) if the service poses a conflict of interest,
such conflict should be disclosed to fiduciary clients
(would be prohibited for ERISA accounts); e) the fiduciary who appoints the investment manager has
an ongoing duty to monitor the manager's use of
soft dollars; and f) the safe-harbor provisions of
Section 28(e) of the Securities Exchange Act of
1934 are the only allowable services available.

2. Policy(ies)/Procedure(s): Should address requirements of TBC-25 in the use of soft-dollar arrangements.

3. Related Bank Policies:

4. Related Issues:

   a. Trust Banking Circular 17 re: soft-dollar purchases

FIDUCIARY COMPLIANCE RISK MANAGEMENT CHECKLIST

COMPLIANCE PROGRAM _____ Check, WP Ref.

or Initials

NUMBER _____ AS OF DATE _____

SECURITIES TRADING ACTIVITIES
(BROKER SELECTION—12CFR9.5)

1. Synoptic: Required policies under this section of Regulation 9 must address the following: a) selection of persons to affect securities transactions, b) reasonableness of commissions paid to execute transactions, c) use of soft dollars under Section 28(e) of the Securities and Exchange Act of 1934, d) allocation of research or other services among accounts, and e) disclosure of these policies and procedures to prospective and existing customers when appropriate.

2. Policy(ies)/Procedure(s): Required as stated above.

3. Related Bank Policies:

4. Related Issues:

   a. soft-dollar arrangements

   b. P&Os 9.4305 and 9.4310 re: broker allocation

   c. TBC 23 re: use of affiliated brokerage only on a not-for-profit basis to avoid self-dealing

FIDUCIARY COMPLIANCE RISK MANAGEMENT CHECKLIST

COMPLIANCE PROGRAM _____   Check, WP Ref.

or Initials

NUMBER _____ AS OF DATE _____

SECURITIES TRADING ACTIVITIES
(TRADE SETTLEMENT AND IDS)

1. Synoptic: Trade settlement occurs when securities are exchanged for cash payment. Most securities trades are settled through the Institutional Delivery System (IDS) of the Depository Trust Company in New York. The SEC and NYSE Rule 387 generally mandate the use of IDS where the bank and broker are either direct or indirect (piggyback) depository participants. Those rules require that participants who do not use IDS must settle on a theoretical settlement date even if the security is not received. For outside directed trades, the use of IDS can cause special problems if an investment advisor initiates a trade without notifying the bank when the bank is the counterparty to the trade. In these cases, the bank should have well-defined communications back to the customer or his or her advisor to determine its authenticity.

2. Policy(ies)/Procedure(s): Should address the monitoring of unsettled (failed) trades to determine the cause. Failed trades could be a sign of broker problems, customer violation of securities laws in not delivering securities or cash for payment, or internal operating problems if the trust records show a position for the security being sold but there is no actual position at the depository. Procedures should also address independent reconciliation of trade tickets to broker confirmations outside of the trader's desk.

3. Related Bank Policies:

4. Related Issues: *OCC Handbook for Fiduciary Activities*, pp. 18-20

FIDUCIARY COMPLIANCE RISK MANAGEMENT CHECKLIST

COMPLIANCE PROGRAM _____   Check, WP Ref.

or Initials

NUMBER _____ AS OF DATE _____

CONFLICTS OFINTEREST/SELF-DEALING
[12 CFR 9.12(a)]

1. Synoptic: Prohibits a bank from INVESTING FIDU-
   CIARY FUNDS in stock, or obligations of, or other
   property acquired from: a) the bank, its directors,
   officers, or employees; b) affiliates of the bank or
   their directors, officers, or employees; or c) property
   acquired from individuals with whom there exists
   such a connection, or organizations in which there
   exists such an interest, as might affect the exercise
   of the best judgment of the bank in acquiring the
   property unless specifically authorized by the governing instrument, local law, or court order.

2. Policy(ies)/Procedure(s): Should address the prohibitions with specific parties noted in (a) as well as
   set up a mechanism to identify any individuals or
   organizations which have a relationship with the
   bank which could affect the best judgment of the
   bank when acting in the best interests of the benefi-
   ciary(ies). Such policies should emphasize the specific authority required, not simply broad or general
   authority that trust instruments often contain. Courts
   have held that such broad authority (often called ex-
   culpatory provisions) in the instrument does not protect the trustee. Where the trustee attempts to
   obtain written authorization from the beneficiaries,
   the policy should require that the bank obtain written authorization from ALL beneficiaries ONLY AF-
   TER it makes a full and complete disclosure of all
   of the material facts and circumstances surrounding

the conflict of interest. Such authorization is inferior authority to the authorization of court, local law, or the instrument.

3. Related Bank Policies:

4. Related Issues: Numerous precedents and opinions, trust interpretations, trust banking circulars, and other pronouncements as well as coordination with other federal statutes, e.g., ERISA and relevant state statutes as referenced within the database.

FIDUCIARY COMPLIANCE RISK MANAGEMENT CHECKLIST

COMPLIANCE PROGRAM_____   Check, WP Ref.

or Initials

NUMBER _____ AS OF DATE _____

CONFLICTS OF INTEREST/SELF-DEALING
[12 CFR 9.12(b)]

1. Synoptic: ' Prohibits a bank from SELLING OR TRANSFERRING ASSETS held in fiduciary accounts to a) the bank, its directors, officers, or employees; b) affiliates of the bank or their directors, officers, or employees; or c) individuals with whom there exists such a connection or organizations in which there exists such an interest, as might affect the exercise of the best judgment of the bank in selling or transferring the property unless i) specifically authorized by the governing instrument, local law, or court order; ii) advised by counsel it has incurred a liability and wishes to relieve itself of that liability; iii) has a defaulted fixed income investment held in a collective investment fund; or iv) where required by regulatory authority.

2. Policy(ies)/Procedure(s): Should address the prohibitions with specific parties noted in (a) as well as set up a mechanism to identify any individuals or organizations which have a relationship with the bank which could affect the best judgment of the bank when acting in the best interests of the beneficiary(ies). Such policies should emphasize the specific authority required, not simply broad or general authority that trust instruments often contain. Where the trustee attempts to obtain written authorization from the beneficiaries, the policy should require that the bank obtain written authorization from ALL beneficiaries ONLY AFTER it makes a full and

complete disclosure of all of the material facts and circumstances surrounding the conflict of interest.

3. Related Bank Policies:

4. Related Issues: Numerous precedents and opinions, trust interpretations, trust banking circulars, and other pronouncements as well as coordination with other federal statutes, e.g., ERISA and relevant state statutes.

FIDUCIARY COMPLIANCE RISK MANAGEMENT CHECKLIST

COMPLIANCE PROGRAM _____   Check, WP Ref.

or Initials

NUMBER _____ AS OF DATE _____

CONFLICTS OF INTEREST/SELF-DEALING
[12 CFR 9.12(c)]

1. Synoptic: Prohibits a bank from investing its fiduciary funds in its own stock, or that of an affiliate, unless lawfully authorized by the governing instrument, local law, or court order. This authority must be specific as to the conflict of interest involved. As a general proposition no general investment powers, however broad, would be authority for the bank to invest in its own stock. However, where the trust instrument in general terms authorizes the trustee to retain investments, the settlor has waived the rule of undivided loyalty as to bank stock received as an original asset of the account.

2. Policy(ies)/Procedure(s): Should specifically prohibit the purchase of own bank/affiliate securities unless specifically authorized by the account's governing instrument, local law, or court order. The policy(ies)/procedure(s) should also address the retention and sale of own bank/affiliate securities and the authorizations and conditions required in order to continually retain these securities.

3. Related Bank Policies:

4. Related Issues:
   a. OCC P&Os 9.300 and 9.3020
   b. OCC Trust Interpretive Letter 193

FIDUCIARY COMPLIANCE RISK MANAGEMENT CHECKLIST

COMPLIANCE PROGRAM _____   Check, WP Ref.

or Initials

NUMBER _____ AS OF DATE _____

CONFLICTS OF INTEREST/SELF-DEALING
[12 CFR 9.12(d)]

1. Synoptic: Allows a bank to sell assets from one fiduciary account to another as long as the transaction is fair to both accounts and if such transaction is not prohibited by the account's governing instrument or local law. It is best to avoid this type of transaction since only assets subject to indisputable valuation without exposing the trust department to criticism by the beneficiary(ies) of one account or the other.

2. Policy(ies)/Procedure(s): Should address when (if at all) an officer is allowed to conduct transactions between trusts. It is probably best to prohibit interaccount transactions in all circumstances. But if a sale(s)/purchase(s) between accounts is conducted, the sale(s)/purchase(s) should be approved by a senior officer or a committee familiar with all the circumstances and facts behind the transaction.

3. Related Bank Policies:

4. Related Issues:
    a. OCC Trust Interpretive Letter 223
    b. OCC P&Os 9.3700 and 9.3710

FIDUCIARY COMPLIANCE RISK MANAGEMENT CHECKLIST

COMPLIANCE PROGRAM _____ Check, WP Ref.

or Initials

NUMBER _____ AS OF DATE _____

CONFLICT OF INTEREST/SELF-DEALING [12 CFR 9.12(e)]

1. Synoptic: Prohibits the loaning of fiduciary funds from one account to another unless it is authorized by the governing instrument from which the loan is made and the loan is not prohibited by local law.

---

2. Policy(ies)/Procedure(s): Should address the conditions (if any) of when loans can be made from one trust account to another trust account or beneficiary(ies). It should specifically state that the loans will be made only when the best interests of beneficiaries of both accounts are met.

---

3. Related Bank Policies:

---

4. Related Issues:

   a. 12 USC 92a(h)

FIDUCIARY COMPLIANCE RISK MANAGEMENT CHECKLIST

COMPLIANCE PROGRAM _____   Check, WP Ref.

or Initials

NUMBER _____ AS OF DATE _____

CONFLICTS OF INTEREST/SELF-DEALING
[12 CFR 9.12(f)]

1. Synoptic: A bank may loan its funds to its trusts and take as security assets of the accounts (except participations in collective investment funds) provided such transaction is fair to the account and it is not prohibited by local law.

---

2. Policy(ies)/Procedure(s): Should address the circumstances and conditions of when a trust will borrow from the bank. The policy(ies)/procedure(s) should specifically state that no loan from a commercial bank to a trust account may be wholly or partially secured by units of participation in the bank's collective investment funds.

---

3. Related Bank Policies:

---

4. Related Issues:
   a. 12 CFR 9.18(b)(8)(i)
   b. OCC P&Os 9.3800, 9.5400, and 9.5405

FIDUCIARY COMPLIANCE RISK MANAGEMENT CHECKLIST

COMPLIANCE PROGRAM _____   Check, WP Ref.

or Initials

NUMBER _____ AS OF DATE _____

CONFLICTS OF INTEREST/SELF-DEALING
OCC TRUST (BANKING CIRCULAR 19)

1. Synoptic: Basic principles of trust law prohibit a corporate fiduciary from purchasing securities that are
   being underwritten by the commercial department of
   the bank, or its affiliates for its fiduciary accounts,
   under the following conditions: (a) absent specific
   authorization in local law, (b) provisions of the governing instrument, or (c) directions in writing by an
   authorized powerholder.

2. Policy(ies)/Procedure(s): Should address the pro
   hibitions noted in the circular, as well as set up a
   mechanism whereby trust investment personnel are
   notified of bank or an affiliate's participation in the
   syndicate. In addition, a mechanism should be established to obtain authority to purchase these
   bonds from the powerholder(s) after a full disclosure
   of the conflict is made to all such powerholder(s).

3. Related Bank Policies:

4. Related Issues:

   a. OCC Trust Interpretive Letters 86 and 188

   b. OCC P&O 9.3261

   c. 12CFR9.12(a)

   d. Competitive Equality Banking Act of 1987, Section 23B(b)(1)(B)(2) appears to require the approval of a majority of the directors of the bank, who are not officers or employees of the bank, to approve the purchase of the bonds.

   e. OCC Banking Bulletin 88-1 entitled "Summary of New Law on Affiliate Transactions"

FIDUCIARY COMPLIANCE RISK MANAGEMENT CHECKLIST

COMPLIANCE PROGRAM _____   Check, WP Ref.

or Initials

NUMBER _____ AS OF DATE _____

CONFLICTS OF INTEREST/SELF-DEALING
[12 USC 92a(h)]

1. Synoptic: Strictly prohibits a bank from making loans to directors, officers, or employees of a national bank from trust accounts administered by that national bank. It should be noted that 12 USC 92a(h) makes no exceptions as to the lending of trust funds to directors, officers, or employees of the bank. Therefore, this statute would prevail over any instrument authority, beneficiary consent, or court order purporting to authorize the transaction. Obligations of directors, officers, or employees which are received in kind do not come within the prohibitions of this statute unless they are renewed or carried past due. Demand loans should be paid within a reasonable time. In an estate this would normally be the usual period of administration. Such obligations should not be transferred by a bank as executor to itself as trustee under the will. Penalties for violating this regulation can be steep (fined up to $5,000 and/or imprisoned up to five years).

2. Policy(ies)/Procedure(s): Should address the strict prohibition against the lending of fiduciary funds to a director, officer, or employee of the fiduciary bank. Policy(ies)/procedure(s) should also address the timely disposition of a loan received in kind in a trust or estate. Any loans received in an agency should probably be distributed out of the account to the principal.

3. Related Bank Policies:

4. Related Issues:

    a. OCC P&Os 9.3650 and 9.3655

    b. OCC Trust Interpretive Letters 17 and 203 OCC
       Interpretive (Commercial) Letter 402

    c. ERISA Section 408(b)(1)

    d. OCC Trust Examining Circular 13

FIDUCIARY COMPLIANCE RISK MANAGEMENT CHECKLIST

COMPLIANCE PROGRAM _____   Check, WP Ref.

or Initials

NUMBER _____ AS OF DATE _____

CONFLICTS OF INTEREST/SELF-DEALING [12 USC 61]

1. Synoptic: This prohibition applies ONLY to a national bank voting the shares of its own bank stock in the election of directors. The regulation provides that the voting of a national bank's own stock held as sole trustee may not be voted unless the account's governing instrument grants to a donor or beneficiary the power to determine how the shares of the bank will be voted and the donor or beneficiary actually directs how such shares will be voted. For co-trusteed accounts, the other co-trustee(s) will be allowed to vote the stock as if they were the sole trustee(s). For all other issues, the bank must vote the stock in accordance with the best interests of the beneficiaries and solely in light of the purposes for which each individual account was created. This prohibition would NOT apply to the voting of bank stock on any other issue or the voting by a national bank stock of its parent holding company or any affiliate on any issue, including the election of directors. The voting of holding company stock would be governed by local law.

2. Policy(ies)/Procedure(s): Should address the proper voting of own bank stock and/or holding company stock in the election of directors as well as other issues. The policy(ies)/procedure(s) should denote that the shares held in trust accounts must be voted in accordance with the best interests of the account beneficiaries and solely in light of the purposes for which each account was created. If it happens that

the bank votes only bank stock (versus holding company stock), then the policies need to specifically address the bank's duty to vote the stock in accordance with the regulation as to the election of directors.

3. Related Bank Policies:

4. Related Issues:

   a. OCC P&O 9.3060

   b. OCC Trust Interpretive Letter 105

FIDUCIARY COMPLIANCE RISK MANAGEMENT CHECKLIST

COMPLIANCE PROGRAM _____   Check, WP Ref.

or Initials

NUMBER _____ AS OF DATE _____

CONFLICTS OF INTEREST/SELF-DEALING
(TRUST BANKING CIRCULAR 23)

1. Synoptic: Absent specific authority in the governing instrument or in local law, a national bank may NOT affect securities transactions for its trust accounts through an affiliated discount broker unless the transactions are performed on a "NONPROFIT BA-SIS." Nonprofit would cover only the costs of affecting the transaction and would not allow the bank to recover any "overhead expense." The opinion also states that if all the beneficiaries of a particular trust are available, competent, apprised of the affiliate relationship, made aware of the fee arrangement, and subsequently give their approval for such transaction, then the use of the affiliate discount brokerage company is permissible. This circular would not apply to custody accounts.

---

2. Policy(ies)/Procedure(s): Should address when an affiliated discount brokerage firm is utilized for both trust and/or custodian accounts. If utilized for trust accounts then the policy(ies)/procedure(s) must state that the fee charged will cover the cost of the transaction and no more, unless specific authority exists in the appropriate governing instrument or local law, proper direction/approval is received from all the proper account powerholders.

3. Related Bank Policies:

_____

4. Related Issues:
    a. OCC Trust Interpretive Letter 6
    b. OCC Investment Securities Letter 33
    c. ERISA Prohibited Transactions Section 406

FIDUCIARY COMPLIANCE RISK MANAGEMENT CHECKLIST

COMPLIANCE PROGRAM _____   Check, WP Ref.

or Initials

NUMBER _____ AS OF DATE _____

CONFLICTS OF INTEREST/SELF-DEALING
(OCC BANKING CIRCULAR 233)

1. Synoptic: The acceptance by a national bank trus-
    tee of ANY financial benefits directly or indirectly
    conditioned on the investment of trust assets in a
    particular investment is prohibited. When selecting
    an investment, a trustee should evaluate the return
    being paid, the composition and length of maturities
    of its portfolio, the fund's management, and all other
    factors relevant to the suitability of the investment
    for the customers. Trustees must not place them-
    selves in a position where their judgments concern-
    ing the optimal investment for trust accounts may
    be influenced by the trustee's receipt of financial
    benefits for selecting a particular investment.

2. Policy(ies)/Procedure(s): Must specifically address
    the unconditional nonacceptance of financial bene-
    fits in the way of rebates or discounts on services
    provided, computer goods or services, seminars
    and travel expenses, or any other financial benefits
    in exchange for investing trust funds in particular in-
    vestments of a service provider (i.e., mutual fund
    company, etc.).

3. Related Bank Policies:

4. Related Issues:

   a. This is one of the "hot topics" that the OCC is
   seeking enforcement actions and reimburse-
   ments on. They are beginning to uniformly make
   banks reimburse trust customers for the services received by the banks and are even making them retroactive to the release of Banking
   Circular 233.

   b. Trust Interpretive Letters 214, 221, 222, 230,
   233, and 234

   c. Bank Interpretive Letters 520, 521, and 558

FIDUCIARY COMPLIANCE RISK MANAGEMENT CHECKLIST

COMPLIANCE PROGRAM _____   Check, WP Ref.

or Initials

NUMBER _____ AS OF DATE _____

CONFLICTS OF INTEREST/SELF-DEALING
(OCC BANKING CIRCULAR 219)

1. Synoptic: National bank fiduciaries cannot accept fees from 12b-1 funds into which trust assets are invested unless, in the case of non-ERISA accounts, specific authority exists for the practice. This would require at least one of the following: a) specific authority in local law, b) specific authority in the governing instrument or affirmative written consents after full disclosure by all parties in interest, or c) court order. This circular specifically states that the OCC may seek enforcement actions (including the possibility of publicly disclosing banks found in violation), as well as require these banks to reimburse the 12b-1 fees to the appropriate accounts.

2. Policy(ies)/Procedure(s): Should address the use of 12b-1 funds in both managed and nonmanaged accounts and the receipt and disclosure of such fees by the bank. The policy(ies)/procedure(s) should at a minimum include the disclosure of all 12b-1 fees collected in an account. This disclosure should be performed at least annually and should be stated in the fiduciary account statement as a separate line item which states in dollars and cents the total amount of such fees attributed to the account since the previous report.

3. Related Bank Policies:

4. Related Issues:

   a. Trust Interpretive Letter 96

   b. SEC Rule 12b-1 (12CFR270.12b-1)

   c. ERISA Prohibited Transactions Section 406

   d. Federal Reserve Regulatory Service (FRRS) 3-1596, dated June 1985

FIDUCIARY COMPLIANCE RISK MANAGEMENT CHECKLIST

COMPLIANCE PROGRAM _____   Check, WP Ref.

or Initials

NUMBER _____ AS OF DATE _____

CONFLICTS OF INTEREST/SELF-DEALING
(TRUST BANKING CIRCULAR 13)

1. Synoptic: Fee concessions to presently employed or
    retired directors, officers or employees, or their im-
    mediate family are allowed, provided such conces-
    sions are consistent with management's marketing
    and profitability objectives. Such concessions must
    be granted under a general policy uniformly applied
    on a nondiscriminatory basis, as part of a compen-
    sation package approved by the board of directors.
    Concessions may not be granted to principal share-
    holders, advisory or honorary directors, or business
    interests of directors, officers, or employees. Exam-
    iners are instructed to criticize trust fee concessions
    in trust departments that are unprofitable.

2. Policy(ies)/Procedure(s): Should address both to
    whom the fee concessions will be granted and what
    type of fiduciary relationships will be eligible for the
    concession. If desirable, this policy can be com-
    bined in the bank's overall compensation policy.

3. Related Bank Policies:

4. Related Issues:

    a. 12CFR9.15

    b. OCC Trust Interpretive Letters 174 and 187

FIDUCIARY COMPLIANCE RISK MANAGEMENT CHECKLIST

COMPLIANCE PROGRAM _____   Check, WP Ref.

or Initials

NUMBER _____ AS OF DATE _____

CONFLICTS OF INTEREST/SELF-DEALING
(TRUST BANKING CIRCULAR 22)

1. Synoptic: The circular recommends various policies and procedures that need to be followed by national bank trust departments wanting to utilize repurchase agreements. Generally, before engaging in repurchase agreements for an account, the bank must ensure that either the account's governing instrument or local law allows the trustee to engage in this type of investment. For employee benefit accounts, the bank must also comply with ERISA Sections 404 and 406. It should be noted that the OCC has taken the position that a repurchase agreement is not the equivalent of an investment in U.S. government securities. Hence, if a particular trust agreement specifies investments are to be made in U.S. government securities, repurchase agreements will not satisfy this requirement. Repurchase agreements should not be purchased from the commercial department unless specifically authorized by the governing instrument, local law, or court order. Under no circumstances may a bank's collective investment fund engage in repurchase transactions with the commercial side of the bank.

2. Policy(ies)/Procedure(s): Should address (at a minimum) the following: a) obtain legal opinion as to the legality of investing in repurchase agreements under local law; b) keep abreast of financial condition of parties that the bank is doing repurchase agreements with; c) repurchase agreements must be en-

tered into pursuant to a written agreement delineating each parties duties and responsibilities; and d) the agreement must describe specific procedures regarding collateral control as contained in the circular. Policy(ies)/procedure(s) must also address the general prohibition from making purchases of such securities from the commercial side of the bank.

3. Related Bank Policies:

4. Related Issues:

    a. 12CFR9.12 and 12CFR9.18(b)(8)(i)

    b. 12CFR9.11, ERISA Section 404, "Prudent Man Rule"

    c. ERISA Prohibited Transaction Exemption 81-8

FIDUCIARY COMPLIANCE RISK MANAGEMENT CHECKLIST

COMPLIANCE PROGRAM _____   Check, WP Ref.

or Initials

NUMBER _____ AS OF DATE _____

CONFLICTS OF INTEREST/SELF-DEALING
(OCC BANKING CIRCULAR 218)

1. Synoptic: This circular deals with the permissibility
   of charging "sweep fees" for the automatic investment of idle cash balances. Banks are encouraged
   to obtain legal opinions in order to determine if the
   charging of sweep fees is permissible under local
   law. Under many state laws the charging of sweep
   fees is not permitted, unless specific authority is
   contained in the governing instrument, court order,
   or valid consents are obtained after full disclosure
   from all parties in interest. For ERISA accounts, this
   issue is governed by a Department of Labor Staff
   Letter, dated August 1, 1986. Generally, under this
   opinion, if a bank does not exercise any fiduciary
   authority or control (i.e., discretion) to cause the
   plan to pay an additional fee for the investment of
   cash, then the bank would be allowed to charge a
   sweep fee and would not be in violation of ERISA
   Section 406(b)(1).

2. Policy(ies)/Procedure(s): Should adequately address the charging (or noncharging) of a sweep fee
   in both personal and employee benefit accounts.
   The policy(ies)/ procedure(s) should include specific
   guidelines to be followed when charging sweep
   fees, the disclosure of such, and the requirement
   that the bank obtain a legal opinion as to the permissibility of charging sweep fees in accordance
   with applicable local law.

3. Related Bank Policies:

4. Related Issues:

   a. 12CFR9.10(a)

   b. Department of Labor Staff Letter dated August 1, 1986 (often referred to as the "Plotkin" letter)

   c. OCC Trust Interpretive Letters 4, 7, 40, and 46

   d. Cash management practices

FIDUCIARY COMPLIANCE RISK MANAGEMENT CHECKLIST

COMPLIANCE PROGRAM _____   Check, WP Ref.

or Initials

NUMBER _____ AS OF DATE _____

COLLECTIVE INVESTMENT FUNDS—GENERAL

1. Synoptic: 12CFR9.18 governs the administration of all collective investment funds (CIFs), regardless of whether the bank is a national bank, state bank, mutual savings bank, etc. In order for a fund to maintain its tax exempt status, it must be operated in accordance with 12CFR9.18. Participation in these funds is limited to certain types of accounts in order to comply with both IRS and SEC regulations, as well as 12CFR9.18. Generally, these funds and their securities are exempt from registration under Section 3(a)(2) of the Securities Act of 1933 and Section 3(c)(3) of the Investment Company Act of 1940. Section 3(c)(11) of the Investment Company Amendments Act of 1970 also excludes CIFs from registration if they consist solely of assets of qualified retirement plans under IRC section 401. It is important to understand when the fund is exempt and when the fund could lose its exemption from registration.

2. Policy(ies)/Procedure(s): Should address the administration of CIFs and pay particular attention to the accounts allowed to participate in such funds, including any prohibitive language in the instrument, the type of account, and the investment philosophy, particularly to comply with 12CFR9.18 and local law.

3. Related Bank Policies:

4. Other Related Issues:

   a. Various state statues, e.g., Common Trust Fund Acts

   b. SEC Rule 180 for participation of H.R. 10 accounts in collective funds, Banking Circular 247, and P&O 9.5990 re: IRA account participation in collective funds

FIDUCIARY COMPLIANCE RISK MANAGEMENT CHECKLIST

COMPLIANCE PROGRAM _____   Check, WP Ref.

or Initials

NUMBER _____ AS OF DATE _____

COLLECTIVE INVESTMENT FUNDS—12CFR9.18(a)

1. Synoptic: 9.18(a) authorizes the establishment of
    two types of CIFs, distinguished primarily by the
    type and tax status of the participating accounts: 1)
    personal or (a)(1) funds where the bank serves as
    trustee, executor, administrator, guardian or custo-
    dian under the Uniform Transfers to Minors Act;
    these funds receive tax exempt status under IRC
    section 584; and 2) employee benefit/group trusts
    or (a)(2) funds which consist solely of assets of re-
    tirement, pension, profit sharing, stock bonus, or
    other trusts which meet the requirements for qualifi-
    cation under IRC section 401; these funds receive
    their tax exempt status from Revenue Ruling 81-
    100 and the bank's relationship can be that of trus-
    tee, agent, or custodian, unlike (a)(1) funds where
    the bank must act in the fiduciary capacity de-
    scribed and not merely as agent or custodian.

2. Policy(ies)/Procedure(s): Should address the eligi-
    bility rules for various account types to ensure the
    fund's tax exempt status is not jeopardized and that
    securities laws are not violated.

3. Related Bank Policies:

4. Related Issues: Special rules apply for H.R.10 (Keogh) Plan and IRA account participation in relation to the need to register the collective funds and in relation to potential violations of the Glass-Steagall Act. SEC Rule 180 deals with H.R. 10s and Banking Circular 247 addresses IRA participation. Also, P&Os 9.5800-9.5810 re: participation of charitable trusts in either (a)(1) or (a)(2) funds under IRC Section 584, and 9.6000-9.6110 re: special opinions on (a)(1) and (a)(2) funds.

FIDUCIARY COMPLIANCE RISK MANAGEMENT CHECKLIST

COMPLIANCE PROGRAM _____   Check, WP Ref.

or Initials

NUMBER _____ AS OF DATE _____

COLLECTIVE INVESTMENT FUNDS—
12CFR9.18(b)(1)-(b)(3)

1. Synoptic: Section (b)(1) states the minimum con-
   tents of the plan which must be in writing and approved by the board of directors and filed with the
   OCC. The plan must include the following: a) statement of investment powers, b) provisions for the allocation of income, c) terms and conditions
   governing admissions and withdrawals, and d) valuation mechanics of the fund (e.g., method for valuation, frequency of valuation, etc.). Section (b)(2)
   requires that (a)(2) funds must be incorporated by
   reference in the plan document since there is a
   commingling of funds of various plans. Section
   (b)(3) requires that all participants own a proportion-
   ate share of all of the assets of the fund.

2. Policy(ies)/Procedure(s): Should address approval
   and filing requirements noted above as well as written fund standards for admissions, withdrawals,
   valuations, and participative shares.

3. Related Bank Policies:

4. Related Issues:

P&Os 9.5000 re: 10-day posting of admissions and withdrawals; 9.5010 re: prohibition of fees for admissions and withdrawals; 9.5011 re: admissions based on market value of fund; 9.5012 re: prohibition of using cost as market value; 9.5015 re: prohibition of charging cost of selling property to withdrawing accounts only; 9.5020 re: prohibition on restricting amounts of withdrawals from fund.

FIDUCIARY COMPLIANCE RISK MANAGEMENT CHECKLIST

COMPLIANCE PROGRAM _____   Check, WP Ref.

or Initials

NUMBER _____ AS OF DATE _____

COLLECTIVE INVESTMENT FUNDS—12CFR9.18(b)(4)

1. Synoptic: This section requires that the bank value the fund, at a minimum, once every three months to allow equitable admissions and withdrawals from the fund. It further states that all admissions and withdrawals will be based on the valuation as of valuation date. Written notices of admissions or withdrawals must be received prior to valuation and no notices can be canceled after the valuation date. It also states that for (a)(2) funds invested in non-readily marketable securities, the bank can require a one-year notice prior to withdrawal.

2. Policy(ies)/Procedure(s): Should address the standards for valuation, notice requirements, and appropriate monitoring devices for adherence. Should also address the method of valuation for assets which do not carry a readily available market value.

3. Related Bank Policies:

4. Related Issues:

   P&Os 9.5000-9.5035 re: admissions and withdrawals

FIDUCIARY COMPLIANCE RISK MANAGEMENT CHECKLIST

COMPLIANCE PROGRAM _____   Check, WP Ref.

or Initials

NUMBER _____ AS OF DATE _____

COLLECTIVE INVESTMENT FUNDS—12CFR9.18(b)(5)

1. Synoptic: This section requires an audit of the fund
    to be performed, at a minimum, each calendar year.
    If the audit is performed by outside accountants, the
    reasonable fee for the audit can be charged to the
    fund. It also requires a financial report to be pre-
    pared at least once every 12 months. (Tax Reform
    Act of 1986 now requires Collective Funds to be
    calendar year taxpayers also.) Section (b)(5) stipu-
    lates the requirements of the financial report. A
    copy of the financial report or a notice of its avail-
    ability must be furnished at no cost to each partici-
    pant in the fund and the cost of printing and
    distributing the report must be borne by the bank.
    Further, the bank is prohibited from advertising or
    publicizing its (a)(1) funds.

2. Policy(ies)/Procedure(s): Should address the re-
    quired audits and annual financial report prepara-
    tion, as well as the charging of fees consistent with
    this section. Should also prohibit advertising (a)(1)
    funds so as not to violate applicable securities laws.

3. Related Bank Policies:

4. Related Issues:

P&Os 9.5100 re: 90-day limit on preparing financial statements; 9.5110 re: allowing comparisons of fund performance with that of general market indices, e.g., S&Ps within annual report; however, it should prohibit comparisons with other bank funds or mutual funds; 9.5112 re: restrictions on information given to prospective customers only for a bona fide promotion of trust services and not for promoting the common trust funds as investments.

FIDUCIARY COMPLIANCE RISK MANAGEMENT CHECKLIST

COMPLIANCE PROGRAM_____   Check, WP Ref.

or Initials

NUMBER_____ AS OF DATE_____

COLLECTIVE INVESTMENT FUNDS— 12CFR9.18(b)(6)-(b)((7)

1. Synoptic: Section (b)(6) states that fund distributions can be made in cash or in kind as long as
   they are made on the same basis to all participants
   withdrawing as of that valuation date. Section (b)(7)
   states that if an investment is withdrawn in kind
   from a fund, and it is not distributed in kind, it must
   be segregated and administered for the benefit of
   all participants in the fund.

2. Policy(ies)/Procedure(s): Should address equitable
   and fair treatment of all participants where fund assets are withdrawn and/or distributed in kind. Policy
   may address that no assets will be withdrawn in
   kind, but rather that cash distributions will be made
   in all cases based on most recent valuation.

3. Related Bank Policies:

4. Related Issues:

   P&Os 9.5200 re: exchange of assets for units

FIDUCIARY COMPLIANCE RISK MANAGEMENT CHECKLIST

COMPLIANCE PROGRAM _____   Check, WP Ref.

or Initials

NUMBER _____ AS OF DATE _____

COLLECTIVE INVESTMENT FUNDS—12CFR9.18(b)(8)

1. Synoptic: This section discusses self-dealing issues, specifically the following: a) no bank shall have an interest in a fund other than in its fiduciary capacity; b) a bank may not lend money to (except for temporary overdrafts), sell property to, or purchase property from the fund; c) a bank cannot invest fund assets in stock or obligations of the bank except for temporary cash management of funds awaiting investment or distribution; d) a bank may not make a loan to the fund or a participating account and take back for security a participation interest in the fund; and e) a bank may purchase from a fund, for its own account, a defaulted fixed-income investment if the bank feels the cost of segregation would outweigh the difference between the market value and its cost plus any interest or penalty involved. (Legal counsel may be needed if there is ambiguity in the definition of default.)

2. Policy(ies)/Procedure(s): Should address the prohibitions of self-dealing as depicted in this section and the requirements for allowable transactions which can only be done under certain circumstances.

3. Related Bank Policies:

4. Related Issues:

P&Os 9.5355 re: prohibition in purchasing repo from commercial side of bank; 9.5360 restricting CD purchases from commercial side to short-term, temporary investments for funds awaiting investment or distribution; 9.5400-9.5410 re: creditor relationships and various prohibitions on pledging fund participations.

FIDUCIARY COMPLIANCE RISK MANAGEMENT CHECKLIST

COMPLIANCE PROGRAM _____   Check, WP Ref.

or Initials

NUMBER _____ AS OF DATE _____

COLLECTIVE INVESTMENT FUNDS—12CFR9.18(b)(9)

1. Synoptic: This section applies only to (a)(1) funds. There is a 10% liquidity limit which prohibits any one account from owning more than 10% of the value of the fund. If more than 10% is owned through direct investment, the participation must be brought down to 10% by the next valuation date. P&O 9.5520 states that if the participation exceeds 15% due to any other reason (e.g., large withdrawals by other accounts), the bank has one year to reduce to the 10% level. There is also a 10% concentration limit which prohibits the fund from investing more than 10% in any one issue (except U.S. guaranteed obligations). If more than 10% is invested through direct investment in any one issue, it must be reduced to 10% by the next valuation date. P&O 9.5515 states that if the 10% is exceeded due to another reason, such as appreciation, when it reaches 15% and stays at that level for six consecutive months, the bank must then reduce to the 10% level. This section also requires that the fund must keep enough cash and readily marketable securities to meet its withdrawal and other liquidity needs.

2. Policy(ies)/Procedure(s): Should address both the liquidity and concentration limits for (a)(1) funds including the proper monitoring procedures against exceeding the limits and proper curtailment.

3. Related Bank Policies:

---

4. Related Issues:

P&Os 9.5510 re: repurchase agreements being subject to 10% restriction even if secured by U.S. government; 9.5512 re: mutual funds being subject to 10% limit even if they are limited to U.S. government; 9.5535 re: CDs, time deposits, etc., not being readily marketable unless they have matured.

FIDUCIARY COMPLIANCE RISK MANAGEMENT CHECKLIST

COMPLIANCE PROGRAM _____ Check, WP Ref.

or Initials

NUMBER _____ AS OF DATE _____

COLLECTIVE INVESTMENT FUNDS— 12CFR9.18(b)(10)-(b)(11)

1. Synoptic: (b)(10) allows for reasonable expenses in servicing a mortgage to be charged against fund income. (b)(11) allows a bank to set up a reserve account for mortgages held in a CIF with the following limits: a) up to 5% of the net income derived from the mortgages during any one accounting period, with an overall limit of 1% of the outstanding principal amount of the mortgages, can be credited to the reserve; and b) at the end of each accounting period, all interest payments on mortgages which are due but unpaid shall be charged against the reserve account and credited to income distributed to participants.

2. Policy(ies)/Procedure(s): Should address all funds which contain mortgages for the proper treatment of income, reserves, and distributable income.

3. Related Bank Policies:

4. Related Issues:

P&Os 9.5700 re: procedures for handling mortgage loans as investments in the fund; 9.5710 re: prohibition against entering into a purchase agreement with the commercial side of the bank for mortgages; 9.5735 re: prohibition against the bank receiving any "points" for servicing a mortgage in the fund; 9.5740-9.5750 re: reserves and segregating mortgages in default.

FIDUCIARY COMPLIANCE RISK MANAGEMENT CHECKLIST

COMPLIANCE PROGRAM_____   Check, WP Ref.

or Initials

NUMBER _____ AS OF DATE _____

COLLECTIVE INVESTMENT FUNDS—12CFR9.18(b)(12)

1. Synoptic: This section requires that the bank maintain exclusive management over the fund. The OCC
   has   disallowed funds where the bank delegated
   management to another party, including GIC funds
   where the fund management was delegated to the
   insurance company or an outside advisor. The section further allows the bank to charge a fee for the
   management of the fund provided that the fee
   charged to each participant when added to other
   fees charged by the bank does not exceed the total
   amount the account would have been charged if it
   was not participating in the CIF.

2. Policy(ies)/Procedure(s): Should address the exclusive management issue, as well the proper level of
   monitoring over fees. Any excess fees must be re-
   imbursed to the account to the extent they exceed
   what would have been the fee in an individually
   managed account.

3. Related Bank Policies:

4. Related Issues:

P&Os 9.5300 re: general rules for charging of fees to the fund; 9.5305 re: fees for fund valuation to be borne by the bank; 9.5310 re: fees for fund amendments to be borne by the bank; 9.5317 re: outside advisor's fees to be borne by the bank unless OCC specifically approves charges to the fund; 9.5330 re: full disclosure of fees charged to the fund; 9.5770-9.5780 and Trust Interpretive Letters 117, 173, 183, 191, and 205 re: exclusive management (many of these interpretations were issued in the context of establishing GIC funds).

FIDUCIARY COMPLIANCE RISK MANAGEMENT CHECKLIST

COMPLIANCE PROGRAM _____   Check, WP Ref.

or Initials

NUMBER _____ AS OF DATE _____

COLLECTIVE INVESTMENT FUNDS—
12CFR9.18(b)(13)-(b)(15)

1. Synoptic: (b)(13) prohibits a bank from issuing cer-
    tificates reflecting a participant's interest on the
    fund. (b)(14) provides that errors made in good faith
    during the normal course of administering the fund
    will not be deemed a violation of this section of the
    regulation if the bank promptly corrects the error af-
    ter its discovery. (b)(15) deals with the estab-
    lishment of short-term investment funds (STIFs) and
    states that STIFs can be valued at cost rather than
    market if the following four requirements are met: a)
    at least 80% of the investments must be limited to
    fixed-income securities which have a maturity date
    not to exceed 91 days; b) the difference between
    cost and anticipated principal value at maturity must
    be accrued on a straightline basis; c) assets must
    be held to maturity under normal circumstances;
    and d) after affecting admissions and withdrawals,
    at least 20% of the fund must consist of cash or
    assets that will mature on the fund's next business
    day.

2. Policy(ies)/Procedure(s): For (b)(13), policy should
    address the issuance of a certificate (especially for
    GIC funds) to avoid violating this subsection as well
    as securities laws. (b)(14) is an allowing subpara-
    graph and no policies or procedures are pertinent.
    For (b)(15), policy should address STIF require-
    ments noted.

3. Related Bank Policies:

4. Related Issues:

P&Os 9.5900-9.5910 re: special opinions on the operation of STIF funds

FIDUCIARY COMPLIANCE RISK MANAGEMENT CHECKLIST

COMPLIANCE PROGRAM _____   Check, WP Ref.

or Initials

NUMBER _____ AS OF DATE _____

COLLECTIVE INVESTMENT FUNDS—
12CFR9.18(c)(1)-(c)(5)

1. Synoptic: This section provides other instances where the bank may invest the assets of more than one account collectively as follows: (c)(1) in shares of a mutual trust investment company; (c)(2) in a single real estate loan, a government obligation, or variable amount note; (c)(3) a "mini CIF" where the total amount of the fund will not exceed $100,000 and the total number of participating accounts will not exceed 100; (c)(4) in any investment specifically authorized by court order or the governing instrument; and (c)(5) in such manner as approved by the OCC (these are commonly referred to as (c)(5) funds and include, among other types, GICs, BICs, and GACs under special circumstances).

2. Policy(ies)/Procedure(s): Under (c)(5) policies/procedure(s) should include obtaining OCC approval for collective investment funds that do not specifically meet any of the other allowing sections of 12CFR9.18.

3. Related Bank Policies:

4. Related Issues:

P&Os 9.5921 re: valuation on option funds; 9.5942-
9.5944 re: special restrictions on ERISA funds for
indicia of ownership on foreign securities funds;
9.5961 re: one-year appraisal requirement for real
estate funds; 9.5980 re: special rules on index
funds; 9.5990 re: IRA fund special SEC problems
(H.R. 10 plans also have special requirements under SEC Rule 180); 9.6200-9.6610 re: opinions on
(c)(1)-(c)(5) funds.

FIDUCIARY COMPLIANCE RISK MANAGEMENT CHECKLIST

COMPLIANCE PROGRAM _____   Check, WP Ref.

or Initials

NUMBER _____ AS OF DATE _____

COLLECTIVE INVESTMENT FUNDS—IRAs AND H.R.10s

1. Synoptic: In P&O 9.6935, the OCC does not object to the commingling of IRAs or H.R.10s (Keogh plans) in collective funds. However, they acknowledge such commingling in collective funds requires compliance with the securities laws. For IRAs, Banking Circular 247 acknowledges that the SEC position for IRAs is that they are general retail accounts and NOT bona fide fiduciary accounts and, therefore, the registration exemption for a fund containing only bona fide fiduciary accounts is not available for any fund containing IRA accounts. Therefore, any fund containing IRA participating accounts must be registered.

For Keogh plans, fund participation may be exempt from registration under the Securities Act of 1933 as an intrastate offering, a private placement, or under SEC Rule 180. If nonresident plan assets are invested, this destroys the intrastate offering exemption; if H.R.10 assets are commingled with Section 401 Qualified Plans, Rule 180 must be satisfied. Section 3(c)(11) of the Investment Company Act of 1940 (as amended by the Investment Company Amendments Act of 1970) excludes from the definition of investment company "tax qualified retirement plans." The problem is that H.R.10 participation interests are NOT exempt from registration under Section 3(a)(2) of the 1933 act. Therefore, the private placement exemption (Section 4(2) of the 1933 act) must be met or Rule 180 (SEC Release 33-6363) must be met to exempt

H.R. 10 participation from registration in a collective fund. Rule 180 requires either of the following: a) the employer is a law firm, accounting firm, investment banking firm, pension consulting firm, or investment advisory firm; or b) the employer obtains investment advice from a qualified person unrelated to the bank, prior to investing the plan assets in the fund.

2. Policy(ies)/Procedure(s): Should address the participation limitations of both IRA and H.R.10 accounts in collective funds to ensure compliance with securities laws.

3. Related Bank Policies:

4. Related Issues: Contained herein

FIDUCIARY COMPLIANCE RISK MANAGEMENT CHECKLIST

COMPLIANCE PROGRAM _____   Check, WP Ref.

or Initials

NUMBER _____ AS OF DATE _____

SECURITIES TRADING PROHIBITIONS
(RESTRICTED SECURITIES RULE 144)

1. Synoptic: Rule 144 is a "safe harbor" for disposing of restricted or control securities under Section 4(1) of the Securities Act of 1933. Depending on whether the seller is or is not an affiliate of the issuer of the securities, there are restrictions on the holding period, volume, and manner of sale, as well as disclosure requirements on the intent to sell the securities.

2. Policy(ies)/Procedure(s): Should address the identification of restricted and control securities within the account base, preferably by identifying these with a special asset type code. Should also address the notice, volume, and holding period requirements to prevent inadvertent sale of such securities in violation of securities laws.

3. Related Bank Policies:

4. Related Issues:

FIDUCIARY COMPLIANCE RISK MANAGEMENT CHECKLIST

COMPLIANCE PROGRAM _____   Check, WP Ref.

or Initials

NUMBER _____ AS OF DATE _____

SECURITIES TRADING PROHIBITIONS
(ANTI-FRAUD RULE 10b-5)

1. Synoptic: This rule is promulgated under the Securities Exchange Act of 1934 and makes it unlawful, using interstate commerce, mail, or any facility of any national securities exchange to: a) employ any device, scheme, or artifice to defraud; b) make any untrue statement of a material fact or to omit a material fact that is necessary to make the statement not misleading; or c) engage in any practice, or course of business which operates or would operate as a fraud or deceit upon any person, in connection with the purchase or sale of any security. The Insider Trading Sanctions Act of 1984 created a more effective deterrent, imposing additional sanctions over and above the disgorgement of profits.

2. Policy(ies)/Procedure(s): Required under 12CFR9.7 (d) and should address strict prohibitions against insider trading (which is a fraud under the act; the fraud being the nondisclosure to the general market) as well as any other action, such as passage of rumors, communication of any nonpublic information passed by brokers, customers, corporate trust employees, commercial bank employees or anyone else. Strict control over any information that might be material, nonpublic information is crucial.

3. Related Bank Policies:

4. Related Issues:

INSTITUTIONAL CUSTODY SERVICES AND SECURITIES LENDING

Over the last decade, custody products have become increasingly desirable to offer for trust departments that have a substantial number of corporate and institutional customers. The essential services provided by this area include: safekeeping of assets, automated trading access by the customer to their portfolio, settlement of trades through the Institutional Delivery System of Depository Trust Company, collection of principal and income, monitoring of bond calls, and automated "sweeps" of uninvested cash.

Further, larger trust departments who have clients interested in the global markets have expanded this product into a "Global Custody Service" which expands the requirements in operating support to include the use of foreign exchange systems, foreign tax laws, multicurrency settlement systems, reporting of gains or losses on foreign exchange, etc. This expansion has also created a

169

need to understand foreign cultures and customs as they relate to trade settlement, custodial "subagenting" to foreign custodians, use of foreign brokers, dealers, and traders as well as an in depth understanding of foreign securities markets and foreign economies. The INHERENT RISK in operating in the global markets intensifies because of the lack of physical proximity between those markets and our own domestic markets.

As an ancillary product to institutional custody services, many trust departments engage in the lending of customer securities at the express authorization of the customer. This activity provides customers with above market returns for the lending of securities and also creates elements of risk because of the nature of the transaction—a credit extension of securities to a third party. The INHERENT RISK in offering this product is the riskiness of the credit extension and the requirements of the securities lending operating support system to control credit evaluations, collateral adequacy, marking the securities lent and the collateral to the market on a daily basis, as well as other recordkeeping requirements unique to this product. Securities lending can also be offered to other products such as employee benefit plan trusteeships, where the bank is also acting as custodian of the securities.

In the residual risk assessment that follows, an operating support risk within the administration risk category is included because it is integral to an understanding of the total risk picture for the securities lending aspect of institutional custody services.

DECISION TO ACCEPT NEW APPOINTMENT

Residual risks associated with the management decision of accepting a new institutional custody appointment include the following:

- Inaccurate recordkeeping due to poor set-up procedures for the new account, specifically: identification of authorized individuals for the movement of securities, identification of brokers the client will be using to execute transactions and therefore, will be settling on an automated basis through the Institutional Delivery System.

- Insufficient policies and procedures with respect to settlement instructions due to the customer having various settlement instructions for different trades or security types which have not been properly documented at set-up time.

- Inadequate policies to determine the customer expectations for services such as the customer wanting sophisticated trading abilities, e.g., trading in the global markets, where the bank does not have the experience or the operating support capabilities to handle this type of transaction.

- Insufficient training of personnel in the use of on-line systems, which are part of the service package offered to the client to record or execute their own trades.

- Lack of adequate policies and procedures for credit evaluations of brokers to whom securities would be lent on behalf of the client, as well as lack of adequate operations support for the securities lending accounting requirements.

- Inadequate policies and procedures for the receipt of verbal instructions and the requirements of written confirmations to authenticate and document the authorization.

- Poor custody operating procedures, particularly in the monitoring of the securities movement to and from outside depositories and the reconciliations with outside depositories. Operations may be bursting at the seams in terms of handling additional new business, or the account size or volume may create significant stress on the system of internal controls.

Controls to mitigate residual risks in accepting new institutional custody appointments include the following:

- Policies and procedures which require account acceptance by all relevant parties that might be affected, e.g., securities lending manager if the client may require securities lending activities; operations if the client may be of the size to create extreme volume stresses in the operating activities, etc.

- Account acceptance checklists that include items such as: securities lending potential, compensation in fees, queries as to whether global markets will be entered, settlement instructions, brokers used, requirements for written instructions and confirmations, instructions when settlement will create an overdraft in the account (e.g., preapproved credit lines), etc.

- Formal approval process by division management after reviewing the checklists and other profile information obtained for the prospective client.

- Policies that require legal review of the custody contract if the bank's already approved contract is modified by the client prior to acceptance.

- Policies that require identification of special services, such as reporting on foreign exchange gains or losses, foreign tax reporting, cash management (treasury) services, etc.

- Policies and procedures which require use of internal cash and securities movement systems that have already been evaluated as having adequate control, e.g., wire transfer systems, letter of credit systems, DTC institutional delivery system, etc.

- Policies and procedures to physically and logically monitor the use of any on-line systems supplied to the customer, e.g., automated trading or cash settlement systems, cash management systems with the ability to initiate wire transfers, etc.

- Policies and procedures which require timely and accurate review of the institutional custody account, at least annually, to determine that the account is being administered properly in accordance with the contract.

ADMINISTRATION ACTIVITIES

Residual risks associated with the administration of institutional custody accounts include the following:

- Client may want to invest in securities beyond the capabilities of the accounting system to properly monitor and control (e.g., foreign securities which may not have readily available prices or for which there is no foreign currency translation support).

- Client may want additional services provided, e.g., securities lending services or automated wire features that the bank is not equipped to offer.

- Volume of transactions or other circumstances may create untimely contributions to the account, excessive errors, loss of securities in movement to/from depository, etc.

- If global markets are used, foreign subagents used for securities movement, cash movement, securities safekeeping, telecommunications support, etc., may not be performing to the extent required to adequately control operational aspects of the account.

- For securities lending programs, brokers used may not meet credit requirements or may not pledge collateral sufficient under the contract.

- Client may not be properly trained or is not controlling properly, access and updating through on-line systems for initiating trades, wires, cash credits to a correspondent account, etc., or the system lacks the proper safeguards against fraudulent or otherwise unauthorized use.

- Securities trades are failing due to lack of clear and proper settlement instructions, unfamiliarity with the settlement systems (particularly if in a foreign market), lack of cash to settle the transaction, lack of a deliverable security due to theft, operational errors, etc., or broker/dealer problems.

- Administration activities may create a situation that puts the custodian in a conflict of interest. Some examples include if the client wants to purchase a security out of the bank's (or affiliate's) underwriting portfolio, or if the client wants to purchase a government security out of the bank's own portfolio, or if the client wants to purchase a foreign security at a certain price which puts the bank in an awkward situation if the foreign custom or culture requires a "greasing of the palms" for the type of transaction the client wants.

Controls to mitigate residual risk in administration activities include the following:

- Policies and procedures to address requests for additional services after an account has been accepted; these should address the level of approval required for any service not originally contracted for in the custody agreement; they should also address situations for which legal counsel should be obtained.

- Procedures should be in place to monitor the flow of transactions to ensure transactions are processed timely and accurately. These procedures should include the use of time stamps to document when instructions are received and monitor the timeliness of processing properly.

- For securities lending programs, the policies and procedures should include those items required in Trust Banking Circular 22, specifically: credit evaluation standards for borrowers; type and adequacy of collateral (cash, letters of credit, and government securities would be acceptable); securities lent and collateral should be marked to market daily; procedures should exist for margin calls; the accounting system should compare market values of lent securities to market values of collateral on a daily basis; and intraday overdrafts or collateral inadequacies should be addressed immediately, etc.

- Policies and procedures should address trade settlement monitoring, including management reporting of failed trades and their reasons for proper action.

- Policies and procedures should address the use of outside agents, domestic or foreign, including criteria to use to select an agent, e.g., fiscal and financial responsibility, insurance coverage, adequacy of internal controls, management oversight of the agent's activities, etc.

- Ethics policies should be in place throughout the organization, particularly in the trust department, and very specifically focusing on international activities where relevant. These policies should address a code of conduct by officers and employees in dealing with customers, the general public, outside agents, and anyone else the bank employee may come into contact with.

- Procedures should exist to monitor any unusual settlement requirements of foreign exchanges for trading operations in the global markets.

- Accounting systems for global securities trading should include a multicurrency feature allowing each side of the transaction to be reflected in the native currency and a currency translation feature to reflect foreign exchange (FX) gains or losses.

CHAPTER SIX

OPERATIONS AND GENERAL MANAGEMENT RISK ISSUES

The first five chapters discuss risks associated with decisions to accept new business, as well as the risks associated with the administration of accounts in each of the five product lines discussed. Where necessary and relevant, we have also attempted to include operational aspects of the risk that go hand in hand with the account administration.

This chapter discusses administrative and operational risk management issues as a whole in the fiduciary services areas. It is broken down into three areas: economic climate, regulatory climate, and operational climate. This section will provide insight toward high-level management risk issues in the trust areas. Finally, Regulatory Compliance Risk Management Checklists are included at the end of this chapter to cover regulatory reporting aspects and the several significant operational issues not discussed elsewhere.

177

The following are items that can be included in an overall checklist of management risk issues over fiduciary activities:

ECONOMIC CLIMATE

Management Risk Issues

How does the economic climate affect this product line? For example: Are bond calls way up because interest rates are low?

How does the economic climate affect my employees? For example: Is there any element of financial hardship in the families of employees who handle negotiable instruments?

How does the economic climate affect my operational support? For example: Have we deferred the purchase of securities lending operational control systems because of a moratorium on capital acquisitions?

How does the economic climate affect our service to customers? For example: Have we deferred or tried to shortcut certain customer services or created control issues because of cost considerations?

How does the economic climate affect our levels of insurance coverage over trust activities or trust assets? For example: Have we decided to self-insure against or raise our deductibles for fiduciary omissions coverage or for property and liability coverage for real estate held in fiduciary accounts?

How does the economic climate affect the planning process for the trust department? For example: How does the trust area fit into the overall strategy of the corporation? What are the business level and profitability goals of the department? Which accounts will we accept and which will we decline?

REGULATORY CLIMATE

Management Risk Issues

Have we properly taken into account Acts of Congress over the last several years that materially affect our handling of trust appointments or specific trust assets? For example: Are we holding any trust assets which could have environmental hazards and associated cleanup costs under CERCLA? Are we holding trust real estate which needs significant improvements to comply with the Americans With Disabilities Act of 1992?

Have we taken the necessary steps to accept our fiduciary responsibilities to participants under ERISA? For example: Do we properly assess our investment management responsibilities on accounts where we are the trustee and there is no registered investment advisor appointed on the account or do we acquiesce to investment decisions made by the employer or other party?

Do we properly understand the potential fiduciary liability for self-dealing situations in light of recent court cases and do we keep abreast of the case law to understand our fiduciary liabilities? For example: Do we understand our duties to make trust cash productive and our duties to protect participants in ESOPs of closely held or nonpublicly traded companies?

Have we properly initiated policies and monitoring procedures to prevent and detect any violations of securities laws, e.g., trading on insider information?

Do we have a mechanism in place for the ongoing monitoring of laws and regulations affecting our book of trust business, e.g., subscriptions, seminars, automated compliance services?

OPERATIONAL CONTROL CLIMATE

Management Risk Issues

Do we properly monitor the use of suspense and other accounts that should only be used as temporary clearing accounts? For example: Is there a mechanism in place to age suspense items which could result in chargeoffs? Is there a mechanism in place to properly report these to management for follow-up?

Do we have knowledge of and control over the various accounting records that should be reconciled to an independent source, e.g., securities held at outside locations; trust cash on deposit at the bank or other locations; suspense accounts; fee clearing accounts; outstanding trust checks; inventories of unissued checks, bonds, and other instruments that cause loss; or mutual fund holdings?

Do we have operational controls over any elements of credit risk within our trust activities, e.g., overdrafts, securities lending programs, participant loans from employee benefit plans, or promissory notes held in fiduciary accounts?

Are our operations and related systems of internal control sufficient to minimize the risk of theft, embezzlement or other fidelity loss, e.g., sufficient documentation and authorization procedures, identification of functions which should be segregated, sufficient reconciliations of records with independent sources, sufficient physical control over property in the vault, decedent's residence, storage locations, etc.?

Are our automated and manual systems and records sufficiently backed up with offsite records through the use of contingency plans to assure that assets and records are not destroyed and that the operation will be able to recover from major problems?

FIDUCIARY COMPLIANCE RISK MANAGEMENT CHECKLIST

COMPLIANCE PROGRAM _____   Check, WP Ref.

or Initials

NUMBER _____ AS OF DATE _____

REGULATORY REPORTING—GENERAL

1. Synoptic: The following filings are often required by bank trust departments: 1) SEC Form T-1 (required when new issue of publicly held corporate debt securities is issued); 2) SEC Form TA-1 (registration as a transfer agent with appropriate bank regulator is required when a major change in relationship takes place); 3) SEC Form TA-2 (reporting activities of a registered transfer agent each August 31); 4) Trustee's annual report (required under the Trust Indenture Reform Act annually as of May 15, by July 15); 5) SEC Forms 3-5 (SEC Form 3 is required after 10% ownership of securities acquired, SEC Form 4 is required on capital changes to securities in SEC Form 3, and SEC Form 5 is an annual statement of beneficial ownership of 10% of securities; 6) SEC Schedule 13D (reporting of acquisition of 5% of issuer shares within 10 days after acquisition); 7) SEC Schedule 13G (reporting by passive investors of 5% ownership in lieu of 13D within 10 days or within 45 days of calendar year end); 8) SEC Schedule 13F (reporting of certain holdings when bank has discretion over more than $100 million in exchange-traded stock quarterly); 9) SEC Form 144 (required upon sale of restricted or control stock); 10) Maritime Administration Form MA-580 (annual certification of vessel or shipyard trusts for continued approval); 11) Treasury Department Form BL-2 International Capital (required to report beneficial interests of foreigners in the United States); 12) Securities Information Center (SIC) Registration Form, Inquiry Form, and Form X-17F-

1A for reporting missing, lost, stolen, and counterfeit securities; 13) Annual Report of Trust Assets (FFIEC 001); 14) Special Report of Fiduciary Activities (National Banks); 15) Reports of Radio and Television Co. holdings under 47CFR73.3615; 16) Reports of Airline Co. holdings under 103CFR245; and 17) Large trader reporting under Rule 13h-1.

2. Policy(ies)/Procedure(s): Should address centralized control point to ensure all filings have taken place.

3. Related Bank Policies:

4. Related Issues: Contained herein

FIDUCIARY COMPLIANCE RISK MANAGEMENT CHECKLIST

COMPLIANCE PROGRAM _____   Check, WP Ref.

or Initials

NUMBER _____ AS OF DATE _____

REGULATORY REPORTING—
ROUTINE FIDUCIARY ACTIVITIES

1. Synoptic: The following filings are required for routine fiduciary activities: a) Annual Report of Trust
   Assets (FFIEC 001) 12/31; b) Special Report of Fiduciary Activities (national banks only) 12/31; c)
   Form 5500 Series for Employee Benefit Plans,
   seven months after close of plan year; d) SEC
   Form TA-1 (required under the Securities Reform
   Act of 1975) registration as a transfer agent with
   appropriate bank regulator; e) Form T-1 when new
   issue of publicly held corporate debt securities is offered (corporate trustee activities); f) SEC Form
   TA-2 Annual Report of a registered transfer agent
   each August 31.

2. Policy(ies)/Procedure(s): Should address the monitoring of schedules for report preparation and instructions for preparation when interpretation
   beyond the Form Package Instructions is necessary.

3. Related Bank Policies:

4. Related Issues:

A review of the *ABA Guide to Trust Department Regulatory Reporting* requirements should be assigned to a trained individual.

FIDUCIARY COMPLIANCE RISK MANAGEMENT CHECKLIST

COMPLIANCE PROGRAM _____   Check, WP Ref.

or Initials

NUMBER _____ AS OF DATE _____

REGULATORY REPORTING—LARGE HOLDINGS AND TRADING ACTIVITY

1. Synoptic: The following reporting is required: a) SEC Schedule 13F quarterly for institutions with $100 million in discretionary assets of exchange traded securities; b) SEC Schedule 13D reporting of acquisition of 5% of issuer shares within 10 days after acquisition; c) SEC Schedule 13G reporting in lieu of 13D for passive investors within 10 days or within 45 days of calendar year end; d) SEC Forms 3-5: SEC Form 3 is required after 10% beneficial ownership of securities acquired, SEC Form 4 is required upon capital changes of securities identified in SEC Form 3, and SEC Form 5 is required within 45 days after issuer's fiscal year annual report (10-k) detailing transactions that were not previously reported (NOTE: These filings are pursuant to Section 16 dealing with persons presumed to be insider, e.g., directors, officers, and 10% securities holders. As such, the bank may have additional reporting compliance responsibilities under new 16(a) if a co-trustee is an insider under Section 16); Rule 13h-1 (proposed) would require reporting of large traders (100,000 shares or $4 million in market value in any 24-hour period) within 10 days of exceeding these thresholds.

2. Policy(ies)/Procedure(s): Should address legal requirements and definitions of "beneficial owners," "insiders" as defined by Section 16, monitoring of reporting requirements where the bank, individual

accounts, or a combination of both, are 10% beneficial owners of securities, as well as proper monitoring where a co-trustee, e.g., is an "insider" as
defined under Section 16. Policy emphasis on legal
counsel is recommended for effective implementation of reporting compliance.

3. Related Bank Policies:

4. Related Issues:

10b-5 Trading on inside information; Section 16 requirements on disgorgement of profits from short or
swing sales and criminal sanctions.

FIDUCIARY COMPLIANCE RISK MANAGEMENT CHECKLIST

COMPLIANCE PROGRAM _____   Check, WP Ref.

or Initials

NUMBER _____ AS OF DATE _____

REGULATORY REPORTING—HOLDINGS OF CERTAIN COMPANIES' SECURITIES

1. Synoptic: There are sanctions and reporting require-
    ments for holding securities of certain types of com-
    panies for the interest of national security. The
    major reporting requirements are as follows: a)
    Maritime Administration Form MA-580 for the an-
    nual certification and approval of holding vessel and
    shipyard trusts; b) Treasury Department Form BL-2
    International Capital to report beneficial interests of
    foreigners in the United States; c) 47CFR73.3615
    reporting requirements for radio, television, and
    other broadcasting company holdings; and d)
    103CFR245 reporting requirements for airline com-
    pany holdings.

2. Policy(ies)/Procedure(s): Should address the identi-
    fication of all companies whose holdings are subject
    to federal sanctions, either holding limitations, re-
    porting requirements, or other sanctions. Should fur-
    ther address all holdings of foreigners in the United
    States. The policies and procedures should empha-
    size the involvement of legal counsel to define and
    interpret the federal statutes and regulations, as
    well as the systemic identification of those persons
    and companies subject to reporting through auto-
    mated system attribute coding.

3. Related Bank Policies:

4. Related Issues:

Should review the *ABA Guide to Trust Regulatory Reporting* and consult with counsel versed in federal laws and regulations pertaining to national security and bank reporting (these reports are not limited to trust activities).

FIDUCIARY COMPLIANCE RISK MANAGEMENT CHECKLIST

COMPLIANCE PROGRAM_____   Check, WP Ref.

or Initials

NUMBER_____ AS OF DATE _____

REGULATORY REPORTING—TRANSACTION ACTIVITY/SECURITIES LOSS

1. Synoptic: Sales of restricted or control stock are re-
    portable on Form 144 under Rule 144 of the Securi-
    ties Act of 1933. Rule 144 imposes limitations as
    "safe-harbor" provisions for trading unregistered
    stock. These limitations include: two- or three-year
    holding requirements (depending on whether the
    seller is an affiliate of the issuer), volume limitations
    on the sale, and disclosure requirements of the in-
    tent to sell such securities. Rule 17f-1 requires the
    reporting of lost, stolen, missing, or counterfeit se-
    curities on Form X-17F-1A, as well as the registra-
    tion of anyone who handles registered securities in
    order to afford protection and indemnification of that
    person if they receive securities previously reported
    as missing, lost, etc.

2. Policy(ies)/Procedure(s): Should address the identi-
    fication of any restricted or control stock that is sub-
    ject to the Rule 144 disclosure requirements to
    prevent violation of securities laws, including possi-
    ble sanctions under the anti-fraud provisions Rule
    10b-5. For missing securities, procedures should
    address Rule 17f-1 requirements to protect the
    bank in the event a customer, bank, transfer agent,
    or depository loses a security, or it is lost in transit,
    or the bank takes in a security that has been pre-
    viously reported as lost, missing, stolen, or counter-
    feit.

3. Related Bank Policies:

4. Related Issues:

   Review of specifics of Form 144 and
   17CFR240.17f-1 (Rule 17f-1) by trained individual
   to determine requirements.

FIDUCIARY COMPLIANCE RISK MANAGEMENT CHECKLIST

COMPLIANCE PROGRAM _____   Check, WP Ref.

or Initials

NUMBER _____ AS OF DATE _____

REGULATORY REPORTING—CORPORATE TRUST ACTIVITIES

1. Synoptic: In addition to SEC Forms T-1, TA-1, and TA-2, corporate trustee activities also create obligations on the trustee for the following: a) to ensure that proper registrations have taken place under the Securities Exchange Act of 1933; b) to report annually on Form TA-6 of its continued eligibility to act as trustee (under Section 310 of the Trust Indenture Reform Act of 1990, the annual report must be filed only if changes have occurred since the last filing); and c) if the bank is a registered transfer agent, to report turnaround noncompliance and failure to meet the requirements for responses to transfer inquiries within the time frames allowed in 17CFR240.17Ad-2 and 17CFR240.17Ad-11.

2. Policy(ies)/Procedure(s): Should address the required reporting by the bank as both corporate trustee and transfer agent under the various statutes and regulations pertaining to this business unit.

3. Related Bank Policies:

4. Related Issues:

   Secondary market disclosure rules currently being formulated.

FIDUCIARY COMPLIANCE RISK MANAGEMENT CHECKLIST

COMPLIANCE PROGRAM _____   Check, WP Ref.

or Initials

NUMBER _____ AS OF DATE _____

REGULATORY REPORTING—TAX ISSUES: REPORTING

1. Synoptic: There are a number of tax reporting issues that the fiduciary has a responsibility for, and
   they are as follows: a) W-9 certification of taxpayer
   identification numbers and certification of tax-exempt treatment, if applicable (under TEFRA); b)
   1099 issuance (A-abandonment of secured property, B-broker proceeds, DIV-dividends, G-govern-
   ment payments, INT-interest, MISC-miscellaneous
   income, OID-original issue discount, PATR-income
   from cooperatives, R-distributions from pensions,
   annuities, IRAs, etc., S-proceeds from real estate
   transactions); c) 5498-IRA information; d) 1041(k-1)
   trust income; e) 1065(k-1) partnership income; and
   f) 1098 Mortgage Interest Statement.

2. Policy(ies)/Procedure(s): Should address identification of reporting responsibilities for the payment of
   income, interest, and informational reports that are
   required under IRS regulations.

3. Related Bank Policies:

4. Related Issues:

FIDUCIARY COMPLIANCE RISK MANAGEMENT CHECKLIST

COMPLIANCE PROGRAM _____   Check, WP Ref.

or Initials

NUMBER _____ AS OF DATE _____

REGULATORY REPORTING—TAX ISSUES: FILING

1. Synoptic: There are a number of tax filings that the fiduciary is responsible for, including the following: a) estimated tax payments each quarter for trusts and after the second calendar year end while an estate is open (IRC Section 6654(c) presents more stringent requirements for estimated tax payments beginning the second quarter of 1992); b) Form 1041 Fiduciary Income Tax Returns for Trusts and Estates; c) Form 706 Estate Tax Return and 706GS Generation-Skipping Transfer Tax Return for testamentary skip transfers; d) Form 709 Gift Tax Return and Generation-Skipping Transfer Tax Return for inter vivos skip transfers; and e) Form 5500 Series Reports for employee benefit plans (or certification of information to the plan administrator if the Form 5500 is filed outside of the trust department).

---

2. Policy(ies)/Procedure(s): Should address timely montoring of the schedule for which returns are to be filed. For the generation skipping tax, strong policies and procedures need to be in place to make determinations as to the need to file and for computational purposes, e.g., calculating the "inclusion ratio" for the taxability of the transfer as well as grandfathering dates.

3. Related Bank Policies:

4. Related Issues:

Collective Investment Fund returns, H.R. 2645 (pro-
posed) on charitable remainder trust beneficiary notifications, 706-QDT reporting for qualified domestic
trusts, various elections such as QTIP within returns, various reportings to IRS, DOL, and PBGC
for employee benefit plans by plan administrator for
which trustee may be acting under the plan.

FIDUCIARY COMPLIANCE RISK MANAGEMENT CHECKLIST

COMPLIANCE PROGRAM_____   Check, WP Ref.

or Initials

NUMBER _____ AS OF DATE _____

TRUST OPERATIONS (GENERAL OBJECTIVES OF REGULATIONS)

1. Synoptic: The Office of the Comptroller of the Currency has published overall objectives for the operations and control of fiduciary activities on page 15 of the *Comptroller's Handbook for Fiduciary Activities*. They include: a) safeguarding fiduciary assets; b) ensuring the accuracy and reliability of accounting data; c) providing timely management and account information; d) maintaining levels of operating efficiency; e) functioning cost effectively; f) ensuring compliance with laws, rules, regulations, and bank policies; and g) accommodating new financial products and services and future growth.

2. Policy(ies)/Procedure(s): Should address the system of controls within operations from an administrative standpoint, e.g., segregation of duties, information security, efficient and effective staffing plans, management information and exception monitoring systems, and the use of operations as a risk management tool.

3. Related Bank Policies:

4. Related Issues:

    a. OCC Risk Assessment addressing risk supervision, particularly pertaining to management exception reports, management planning over segregation of duties, and other administrative controls.

FIDUCIARY COMPLIANCE RISK MANAGEMENT CHECKLIST

COMPLIANCE PROGRAM _____   Check, WP Ref.

or Initials

NUMBER _____ AS OF DATE _____

TRUST OPERATIONS (ACCOUNTING AND CONTROL)

1. Synoptic: Regulation 12CFR9.8 Books and Ac-
    counts stipulates that fiduciary records will be kept
    separate and distinct from other bank records and
    will contain full information relative to each account.
    It also requires an adequate record of pending liti-
    gation and specifies minimum three year retention
    over pertinent records. In addition, P&O 9.2000
    specifies the basic accounting controls, including: a)
    account asset and cash ledger controls, b) reconcili-
    ation of assets to issuer (CUSIP) control totals, c)
    segregation of assets by type, d) frequency of rec-
    onciliations, and e) account tickler and synoptic in-
    formation among others. P&O 9.2020 specifies the
    minimum level information that should be contained
    on automated files to affect the basic control objec-
    tives. P&O 9.2021 requires remote terminal authen-
    tication techniques be employed to access records.

2. Policy(ies)/Procedure(s): Should address the mini-
    mum accounting control levels required, reconcili-
    ation frequency over cash and asset ledgers,
    outside depositories, suspense and other house ac-
    counts, and input/output controls over file mainte-
    nance changes, e.g., pricing, remittance schedules,
    etc.

3. Related Bank Policies:

4. Related Issues:

FIDUCIARY COMPLIANCE RISK MANAGEMENT CHECKLIST

COMPLIANCE PROGRAM _____   Check, WP Ref.

or Initials

NUMBER _____ AS OF DATE _____

TRUST OPERATIONS (PRINCIPAL AND INCOME ALLOCATION)

1. Synoptic: For trust accounts, there is a unique and distinguishing feature in the accounting for the property interest an individual has in the account's cash position. A separation of income cash from principal cash is required because different parties in interest to the trust may have different property rights to each type of cash. The Uniform Principal and Income Act (as revised) has been adopted by most states and governs which category of cash receipts and disbursements fall into. Fiduciary personnel should be knowledgeable regarding the requirement for allocating principal and income based on the account relationship, as well as the type of receipt or disbursement.

2. Policy(ies)/Procedure(s): Should address the specific requirements of principal and income allocation under the Uniform Principal and Income Act specifically relating to fees, depreciation, depletion, special dividends (e.g., returns of capital), and other capital changes—stock splits, stock dividends, rental receipts from real property, etc.

3. Related Bank Policies:

4. Related Issues:

FIDUCIARY COMPLIANCE RISK MANAGEMENT CHECKLIST

COMPLIANCE PROGRAM_____   Check, WP Ref.

or Initials

NUMBER _____ AS OF DATE _____

TRUST OPERATIONS (CASH ISSUES)

1. Synoptic: A trustee has the duty to make trust cash productive; however, a receptacle account is normally needed to house cash receipts pending investment or distribution. This is usually facilitated by having one large DDA account (often called the Trust Department DDA) on the commercial side of the bank. P&O 9.2007 requires reconciliation of this account to the individual trust account cash ledgers each time the cash position is updated. In addition, even though the total in the DDA account is positive an individual trust account cash balance may be negative, representing an overdraft for the account. As with any overdraft cash balance on the bank's books, a trust account overdraft must be funded (or brought to a .00 balance). The bank must be cautious not to fund trust account overdraft balances with cash balances of other trust accounts (which would be a violation of 12CFR9.12(e) interaccount loans), but rather to fund these from the bank balance sheet (or the trust company's balance sheet if a trust company with separate capital is involved). Also, the charging of interest on the overdraft would be a self-dealing transaction if the bank had discretion over the account and created the overdraft.

2. Policy(ies)/Procedure(s): Should address the required reconciliations as well as the overdraft issue, specifically the extension of credit and funding at account level.

3. Related Bank Policies:

4. Related Issues:

    a. OCC Risk Assessment in the identification of
       risk attribute; credit risk should be identified and
       mitigated with control. Required OD approvals
       should be put in place upon reports prepared by
       operations by Officer Code. Report should in-
       clude overdraft amount, officer, and duration of
       overdraft. Completion should include full expla-
       nation of overdraft reason, corrective action, and
       authorized management approval. Overdrafts
       outstanding beyond certain duration should be
       identified to senior management attention.

FIDUCIARY COMPLIANCE RISK MANAGEMENT CHECKLIST

COMPLIANCE PROGRAM _____   Check, WP Ref.

or Initials

NUMBER _____ AS OF DATE _____

TRUST OPERATIONS (REPORTING OF LARGE CASH TRANSACTIONS)

1. Synoptic: The Bank Secrecy Act of 1970 was enacted to discourage the use of currency in illegal
   transactions and to identify unusual or questionable
   transactions that could aid in investigations.
   31CFR103 contains extensive reporting and recordkeeping requirements to accomplish these objectives. The regulations require each financial
   institution to file IRS Form 4789 for any transaction
   in currency of more than $10,000. Also included are
   bearer instruments, such as bearer bonds. Trust department transactions that could be subject to the
   reporting include: cash funding, estate inventories
   which turn up currency in the residence or safe deposit box, closely held business deposits, or transactions involving bearer bonds.

2. Policy(ies)/Procedure(s): Should address the monitoring and reporting requirements for all transactions subject to reporting. In addition, should
   specifically be addressed at administration level
   where administrator takes possession of currency
   from settlor or from a testator's estate.

3. Related Bank Policies:

4. Related Issues:

   Laws and regulations 31USC5311; 12USC1829b;
   BC 49; BC 67; BC 99; BC 106; BC 193; *OCC
   Handbook for Fiduciary Activities*, p.21

FIDUCIARY COMPLIANCE RISK MANAGEMENT CHECKLIST

COMPLIANCE PROGRAM _____   Check, WP Ref.

or Initials

NUMBER _____ AS OF DATE _____

TRUST OPERATIONS (SECURITIES DEPOSITORIES)

1. Synoptic: Generally, marketable securities are eligi-
    ble to be held at an outside depository unless pro-
    hibited by the instrument or local statute. The
    central depositories normally used are Depository
    Trust Company of New York (DTC) or Midwest De-
    pository Trust Company. For securities not eligible
    for deposit at DTC, the bank can register the securi-
    ties in its own nominee name, unless prohibited by
    the instrument or local statute. The nominee is a
    partnership name and any nominee names should
    be registered with the American Society of Corpo-
    rate Secretaries to prevent duplication of names
    and possible confusion as to who owns the securi-
    ties. The partnership agreement should be author-
    ized by the board of directors, and the partners and
    various authorized individuals who sign certificates
    and other documents should be reviewed peri-
    odically to ensure they are current.

---

2. Policy(ies)/Procedure(s): Should address the use of
    depositories, including authorization to use, evalu-
    tion of the internal controls within the depository, in-
    surance coverage of the depository, and recon-
    ciliations of securities positions.

3. Related Bank Policies:

4. Related Issues:

   OCC Handbook for Fiduciary Activities, pp. 17-18

FIDUCIARY COMPLIANCE RISK MANAGEMENT CHECKLIST

COMPLIANCE PROGRAM _____ Check, WP Ref.

or Initials

NUMBER _____ AS OF DATE _____

TRUST OPERATIONS (SHAREHOLDER COMMUNICATIONS ACT OF 1985)

1. Synoptic: The Shareholder Communications Act of 1985 amended Section 14(b) of the Securities Exchange Act of 1934 to subject any entity that exercises fiduciary powers (such as banks) to the same proxy dissemination requirements as broker-dealers. The SEC adopted Rule 14b-2 and amended Rules 14a-1, 14a-13, 14c-1, and 14c-7 to implement the provisions of the Shareholder Communications Act. These amendments govern the following: a) the process by which registrants (issuers of registered securities) communicate with the beneficial owners of securities registered in the name of a bank, association, or other entity that exercises fiduciary powers; and b) the proxy processing activities of banks.

2. Policy(ies)/Procedure(s): Should address identification of beneficial owners; identification of which beneficial owners object to the disclosure of their beneficial ownership of securities if requested by the issuing company; documentation for the customer's objection (for accounts opened after 12/28/86). The policy should also cover proxy processing activities under the Act, specifically responding to issuing company within seven days for proxy processing material for beneficial owners and forwarding of such proxy material within five days to the beneficial owners (date/time stamp required).

3. Related Bank Policies:

4. Related Issues:

    a. Proxy processing for employee benefit plans of respondent banks which are exempt from the Shareholder Communications Act. Proxy processing procedures for employee benefit plans should require that the investment advisor vote unless specifically prohibited, in which case the bank, as trustee, should vote in the best interests of plan participants.

INTERPRETING THE COMPTROLLER OF THE CURRENCY'S RISK ASSESSMENT METHODOLOGY FOR TRUST ACTIVITIES

BACKGROUND OF RISK ASSESSMENT TECHNIQUES IN INTERNAL AUDIT

While the 1970s and 1980s were decades of certain excesses in the financial services industry, the 1990s will clearly be a decade of "squeezing out" these excesses. Historically, this has meant that nonprofit center staff areas such as internal auditing bear a large portion of the austerity programs which companies implement to execute the "squeezing" strategy.

However, when internal auditing has been told to tighten its belt while continuing to crank through the audit program with the same scope and coverage, there are consequences. Either the auditing effort becomes more efficient, or significant business activities are left unaudited or "glossed over" as the result of a lack of manpower.

Efficiency techniques that have blossomed over the last several years include the use of automated tools, e.g., generalized and specific audit software, electronic workpapers, automated audit report writing systems, and other tools based on enormous technological strides made in the last decade. But one of the most important changes internal auditors have made over the last several years has been in the area of risk assessment.

Clearly, there have been struggles in the auditing world on how to design and implement a risk assessment program. In the 1960s, IBM and a host of auditors suggested a risk assessment philosophy in the area of systems. A complex set of formulas based upon the estimated dollar loss of a given event (such as the destruction of the data center) times the probability of the event happening over a certain time frame, gave rise to an annual loss value that could be placed on that event.

Many have seen the "RISK MATRICES," "WEIGHTING SYSTEMS," "INHERENT AND RESIDUAL RISK METHOD," and other risk assessment tools, some of which work better than others. The good ones work well based on a combination of: 1) the quality of the analysis that went into the design of the RISK MODEL, 2) the understanding of the objectives of the RISK MODEL by the auditors using it, 3) the clarity of the RISK MODEL in its implementation, 4) the objectivity of the auditors using it (not predetermining the results to fit a certain value of the model), and 5) the ability of the RISK MODEL to be flexible when new variables are introduced and stand the test of time.

In the fiduciary activities areas (such as trust and estate administration, investment management, custody, retirement services, bond indenture trusteeships and agencies, etc., as well as the associated operating areas, such as tax, remittance processing, securities movement, income collection, etc.), many internal auditors have devised risk models to attempt to allocate resources toward "high-risk" areas. The types of risk vary by model; however, the risks can typically be classified along the following characteristics:

fraud or embezzlement
loss or destruction of trust assets
loss of revenue or excessive cost
incorrect decision-making
competitive disadvantage
unacceptable accounting
inaccurate account recordkeeping
violation of law or regulatory sanction

THE OCC INTRODUCES ITS RISK ASSESSMENT PROGRAM

For many of the same reasons that internal auditing developed risk assessment approaches in the last several years—cost-cutting, improving efficiency and effectiveness of audit and, generally, trying to fit 20 pounds of audit effort into a 10 pound bag of audit time—the Office of the Comptroller of the Currency, OCC, has now developed a risk assessment program and is currently testing it during its examinations.

The OCC's philosophy is that risk management must be a management priority and management accountability for risk is crucial to the OCC's examination findings. The OCC places great emphasis on the following factors during its risk assessment of fiduciary activities:

management planning processes
management policies, standards, and procedures
exception monitoring systems for management
performance monitoring systems for management
quality of internal trust audit effort

> type and quality of management information systems
> fiduciary administration review processes

These factors are, indeed, very focused on the role that the board of directors and management play in the oversight of fiduciary activity risk. The OCC divides its analysis into four major types of risk assessment attributes that are looked at during the course of the examination: risk tolerance, risk identification, risk supervision, and risk monitoring. Each is described below.

Risk Tolerance

Within this attribute, the OCC addresses the fiduciary planning process and the criteria used to develop the plans. Specifically, the OCC suggests that management should develop tactical (one year) and strategic (three to five year) plans which are: a) **approved** by the board of directors or committee thereof; b) **specific** as to operating and financial objectives; c) **updated** at least annually; and d) **incorporated** into the corporate planning process.

In addition, the OCC evaluates the criteria used in establishing the plans and the relative impact, in management's estimation, of each of the criteria within the plans. The criteria looked for by the OCC include the following:

> **competitive environment**
> **impact on earnings**
> **expertise and experience requirements of staff**
> **operations capability and limitations**
> **legal and regulatory issues**
> **marketing research and/or customer survey results**

Another area the OCC addresses in the risk tolerance attribute is the **adequacy, proper approval, timeliness,** and **staff awareness** of **policies,** as well as the adequate reporting of deviations from such policies. The policies should include each of the following functional areas of fiduciary activities:

conflicts of interest and self-dealing
personal trust and estate administration
corporate trust administration
fiduciary operations
employee benefit administration
fiduciary investment management
collective investment funds

The last area the OCC covers in the risk tolerance attribute involves **managing** the **nature** of the **fiduciary account** population, to prevent **undue risks** in the administration of fiduciary account relationships. Specifically, the OCC looks for the following: a) **account acceptance standards**; b) **proper review** of duties against the **established standards**; c) **proper approval** of fiduciary appointment by board of directors, designated committee, or **joint** approval by more than one officer; and d) **pricing policies** to match compensation against **above-normal account activity, administrative**, or **investment risk**.

Risk Identification

This attribute focuses primarily on potential losses that could be incurred within the fiduciary areas and the management accountability for judging their magnitude and securing adequate protection against such losses.

In the first portion of the risk identification attribute, the OCC suggests that management put in place a formal process to do the following:

1. **Identify** the nature and amount of any **potential fiduciary losses**.
2. **Establish** a **loss reserve**, as appropriate, based upon expected losses.

3. **Determine** the **factors** to be used to predict losses (e.g., actual, pending or threatened litigation, out of balance or unreconciled ledger balances, historical losses, etc.).
4. **Obtain senior management** and/or **board approval** of the amount (including $0) to be placed in the **loss reserve** (noted in 2. above), at least on an annual basis.

Under this attribute, the OCC reviews the amount in the loss reserve from fiduciary activities as well as the factors used by management to establish the reserve to assess the reasonableness of management's identification of potential losses.

The second portion of the attribute deals with fiduciary **insurance coverage.** Specifically, the OCC is interested in: a) **management review** of policy coverage at least annually; b) **determination** of need for **fiduciary errors and omissions** coverage and, if not needed, whether there is a "self-insurance" program or equivalent coverage under a different policy; and c) **senior management's involvement** in the **assessment** and **approval** of fiduciary insurance coverage.

Risk Supervision

The risk supervision attribute evaluated by the OCC deals primarily with the day-to-day management responsibilities within the fiduciary areas. The first aspect of risk supervision relates to account administration. The OCC assesses the level of annual account review required by Regulation 9.7 over the following account types:

Personal Trusts — Discretionary
Personal Trusts — Nondiscretionary
Employee Benefit Trusts — Discretionary
Employee Benefit Trusts — Nondiscretionary
Managed Agency Accounts
Estates, Conservatorships, Other Court Accounts

Corporate Bond Trustee Accounts
Other Fiduciary Accounts

During their assessment, the OCC uses factors such as: a) **accuracy** of account synoptic information; b) **documentation, clarity, and accuracy** of the established investment objective in relation to the trust or agency document; c) investment practice **consistency** with stated investment objectives; and d) any other **significant fiduciary duties** such as special asset administration (closely held business interests, real estate property, etc.) to evaluate the adequacy of the review process.

The second factor in the risk supervision attribute reflects the level of **management reports** available and the OCC queries as to whether management or the board of directors use such reports in their **oversight of fiduciary activities**. Examples of such reports used by management or the board would include:

Overdraft and Large Cash Balance Reports
New and Closed Account Reports
Fiduciary Revenue and Expense Reports
Product Profitability Reports
Report of Account Reviews and Results
Pending Litigation Reports
Fiduciary Charge-Off Reports
Regulatory Compliance Reports
Customer Complaint Reports
Failed Trade Reports
Suspense and Other Operational Exception Reports
Securities Position/Depository Reconciliation Reports

The final factor the OCC uses in evaluating the risk supervision attribute is the **extent** and **adequacy** of **operational systems** and **controls** to **ensure proper attention** is given to the **management of risk** in the conduct of fiduciary activities.

Risk Monitoring

The last attribute the OCC evaluates is in the area of risk monitoring. It is here that the OCC keys in on the **trust auditing** and **regulatory compliance** functions and their quality. The OCC carefully considers the following factors in assessing the adequacy of management's risk monitoring attribute:

- Whether the **trust auditing** function is performed by **specialists, generalists**, or a **combination** of various backgrounds.

- The **size, experience, training,** and **overall credentials** of the fiduciary audit staff.

- The **scope, frequency,** and **comprehensiveness** of the **internal trust audit program,** taking into consideration the **depth** of any **risk assessment** programs in place as well as the timeliness of required audit procedures, e.g., **verification of assets, administrative account reviews,** etc.

- The **frequency, scope,** and **audience** of fiduciary activity **audit reports,** taking into consideration the **comprehensiveness** of coverage, the significance of **findings** reported, and the **level of management** to which the report is addressed (particularly focusing on distribution to the **fiduciary committee** and **fiduciary audit committee** of the board of directors).

- **Fiduciary audit committee involvement** in the audit process, particularly in the **planning process,** zeroing in on the committee's use of the **internal fiduciary auditors, outside fiduciary audit consultants, external auditors trained** in **fiduciary activities risks,** and others to determine the **adequacy** of the **fiduciary audit program.**

- The methods used to promote **compliance with laws, regulations and internal policies,** including the appointment of a **fiduciary compliance officer, fiduciary compliance training,** the use of **fiduciary compliance** as a measurement in the **employee appraisal process,** and the process to **stay updated** with **new** and **changing requirements.**

- The **level and independence** of **compliance testing** performed over **fiduciary laws, regulations,** and **internal policies.**

The questionnaire which the OCC uses in the Risk Assessment process follows:

Comptroller of the Currency
Administrator of National Banks

FIDUCIARY ACTIVITIES SURVEY

Company/Bank Name: _____

City, State: _____

Note: This survey is to be prepared on a corporate (consolidated) basis unless otherwise directed. If there are any deviations for individual banks, please indicate on the survey. Please circle **ALL** appropriate answers for your institution.

Please indicate who prepared responses to the survey:

Name: _____

Title: _____

Telephone Number: _____

Company/Bank Name: _____

RISK TOLERANCE

1. The fiduciary planning process includes:
   a. Yes No   Short-term financial plan
   b. Yes No   Short-term strategic or operating objectives
   c. Yes No   Action plans designed to achieve stated goals
   d. Yes No   Long-term (three-to-five-year) strategic or financial plans
   e. Yes No   Incorporation into overall corporate planning
   f. Yes No   Review and approval by the board or a board-level committee—Bank or Trust Company
   g. Yes No   Review and approval by the board or a board-level committee—Holding Company
   h. Yes No   Updated at least annually

2. What risk factors are incorporated into the fiduciary planning Process? (on a scale of 1 to 5, with 1 indicating little or no impact, and 5 indicating substantial impact.)
   a. 1 2 3 4 5 Competition
   b. 1 2 3 4 5 Impact on earnings
   c. 1 2 3 4 5 Expertise requirements
   d. 1 2 3 4 5 Operational capability
   e. 1 2 3 4 5 Legal/Compliance issues
   f. 1 2 3 4 5 Customer survey results
   g. 1 2 3 4 5 Other (please describe)

   _____
   _____
   _____

Company/Bank Name: _____

3. Do specific policies cover each functional area of Fiduciary Activities?

   a. Yes No   General fiduciary policies, including Conflict of Interest and Self-Dealing

   b. Yes No   Personal Trust

   c. Yes No   Corporate Trust

   d. Yes No   Fiduciary Operations

   e. Yes No   Employee Benefit Administration

   f. Yes No   Fiduciary Investments

   g. Yes No   Collective Funds

   h. Yes No   Other (please describe)

   _____
   _____
   _____

4. Is the adequacy of overall Fiduciary Policies reviewed and approved at least annually by the:

   a. Yes No   Board of Directors—Holding Company

   b. Yes No   Board of Directors—Bank or Trust Company

   c. Yes No   Trust Committee

   d. Yes No   CEO—Holding Company

   e. Yes No   CEO—Bank or Trust Company

   f. Yes No   Senior Trust Officers Committee

   g. Yes No   Senior Trust Officer

   h. Yes No   Other (please describe)

   _____
   _____
   _____

Company/Bank Name: _____

5. Are procedures in place which are designed to assure that affected personnel are familiar with fiduciary policies?

   a. Yes No

6. Processes used by management to identify instances where fiduciary practice deviates from policy include:

   a. Yes No   Fiduciary managers are required to monitor and report on policy conformance

   b. Yes No   Internal compliance reports

   c. Yes No   Fiduciary audit reports

   d. Yes No   Other (please describe)

   _____

   _____

   _____

7. Processes used to control the quality and nature of fiduciary accounts accepted include:

   a. Yes No   Pre-acceptance review by an authorized committee

   b. Yes No   Joint approval by more than one officer is required

   c. Yes No   Pre-acceptance checklists are used which cover various fiduciary account types

   d. Yes No   Fiduciary policies establish acceptance standards

   e. Yes No   Flexible pricing policy provides for increased compensation for above-normal risks (i.e., operational risk, investment risk, and administrative risk)

   f. Yes No   Other (please describe)

   _____

   _____

   _____

Company/Bank Name: _____

RISK IDENTIFICATION

8. Is fiduciary insurance coverage formally assessed annually?

   a. Yes No

9. Has fiduciary errors and omissions insurance coverage been obtained?

   a. Yes No

   If NO, has the bank:

   b. Yes No   Obtained other equivalent coverage?

   c. Yes No   Established a fiduciary self-insurance program?

   d. Yes No   Formally decided not to insure?

   e. Yes No   Other (please describe)

   _____

   _____

   _____

10. Who is involved in the assessment and approval of fiduciary insurance adequacy?

    a. Yes No   Board of Directors—Holding Company

    b. Yes No   Board of Directors—Bank or Trust Company

    c. Yes No   Trust Committee

    d. Yes No   CEO—Holding Company

    e. Yes No   CEO—Bank or Trust Company

    f. Yes No   Senior Trust Officers Committee

    g. Yes No   Senior Trust Officer

    h. Yes No   Bank or Holding Company Risk Management Officer/Department

Company/Bank Name: _____

   i. Yes No   Other (please describe)

_____

_____

_____

11. Is any formal process in place to identify potential fiduciary losses and establish fiduciary loss reserves, similar to the reserve for possible loan losses?

   a. Yes No

If YES, the factors considered during the evaluation of fiduciary loss reserve adequacy include:

   b. Yes No   Litigation pending or threatened

   c. Yes No   Operational problems, including out-of-balance conditions or other system deficiencies

   d. Yes No   Analysis of historic fiduciary losses

   e. Yes No   Other (please describe)

_____

_____

_____

Frequency of evaluation

   f. Yes No   On an "as needed" basis

   g. Yes No   Quarterly

   h. Yes No   Annually

Officers or Committees involved

   i. Yes No   Board of Directors—Holding Company

   j. Yes No   Board of Directors—Bank or Trust Company

   k. Yes No   Trust Committee

   l. Yes No   CEO—Holding Company

Company/Bank Name: _____

    m. Yes No   CEO—Bank or Trust Company

    n. Yes No   Senior Trust Officers Committee

    o. Yes No   Senior Trust Officer

    p. Yes No   Other (please describe)

    _____

    _____

    _____

12. What is the amount of any reserve for potential fiduciary losses currently on the bank's books?

    a. Yes No   None

    b. Yes No   Less than $1 million

    c. Yes No   Between $1 million and $5 million

    d. Yes No   Between $5 million and $10 million

    e. Yes No   More than $10 million

RISK SUPERVISION

13. Is a formal fiduciary new product/service review (pre-implementation) process in place?

    a. Yes No

    If YES, what bank disciplines are included?

    b. Yes No   Marketing

    c. Yes No   Operations

    d. Yes No   Audit

    e. Yes No   Legal/Compliance

    f. Yes No   Investment Management

Company/Bank Name: _____

g. Yes   No   Other (please describe)

_____
_____
_____

14. Fiduciary account types which are reviewed at least annually by a designated committee include:

a. Yes   No   Personal Trusts—Discretionary

b. Yes   No   Personal Trusts—Non-discretionary

c. Yes   No   EB Trusts—Discretionary

d. Yes   No   EB Trusts—Non-discretionary

e. Yes   No   Managed Agency Accounts

f. Yes   No   Estates, Conservatorships, etc.

g. Yes   No   Corporate Bond Trustee Accounts

h. Yes   No   Other (please describe)

_____
_____
_____

15. Factors assessed during fiduciary account reviews include:

a. Yes   No   Accuracy of synoptic information

b. Yes   No   Propriety of established investment objective

c. Yes   No   Conformance of investments with established investment objective

d. Yes   No   Other (please describe)

_____
_____
_____

Company/Bank Name: _____

16. Reports used by Management for oversight of Fiduciary Administration:

 a. Yes No Overdraft report

 b. Yes No Large cash balances report

 c. Yes No New accounts report

 d. Yes No Closed accounts report

 e. Yes No Fiduciary revenue and expense report

 f. Yes No Margin analysis by product line

 g. Yes No Outside vendor profitability analysis (Trustcompare, OCC Trust Activities Reports, etc.)

 h. Yes No Report of accounts reviewed and results of review

 i. Yes No Pending litigation report

 j. Yes No Fiduciary charge-off report

 k. Yes No Report of compliance activity and results

 l. Yes No Customer complaint report

 m. Yes No Failed trade report

 n. Yes No Operational exception report

 o. Yes No Suspense account reports: uncollected or un-cleared items, etc.?

 p. Yes No Securities position report/reconcilement

 q. Yes No Other (please describe)

_____

_____

_____

17. Reports presented to the board (or board-level committee) for oversight of Fiduciary administration:

 a. Yes No Overdraft report

Company/Bank Name: _____

   b. Yes No   Large cash balances report

   c. Yes No   New accounts report

   d. Yes No   Closed accounts report

   e. Yes No   Fiduciary revenue and expense report

   f. Yes No   Margin analysis by product line

   g. Yes No   Outside vendor profitability analysis (Trustcompare, OCC Trust Activities Report, etc.)

   h. Yes No   Report of accounts reviewed and results of review

   i. Yes No   Pending litigation report

   j. Yes No   Fiduciary charge-off report

   k. Yes No   Report of compliance activity and results

   l. Yes No   Customer complaint report

   m. Yes No   Failed trade report

   n. Yes No   Operational exception report

   o. Yes No   Suspense account reports: uncollected or uncleared items, etc.?

   p. Yes No   Securities position report/reconcilement

   q. Yes No   Other (please describe)

   _____
   _____
   _____

18. Is any system in place for categorizing individual fiduciary accounts by risk level or complexity to assist in managing officer workloads, etc.?

   a. Yes   No

Company/Bank Name: _____

RISK MONITORING

19. Describe your institution's fiduciary auditors:
    a. Yes No   Fiduciary audits performed by staff of fiduciary specialists
    b. Yes No   Staff of financial audit generalists performs fiduciary audits
    c. Yes No   Combination of fiduciary specialists and financial generalists perform fiduciary audits
    d. Yes No   Other (please describe)

    _____

    _____

    _____

    Size of fiduciary audit staff
    e. Yes No   None
    f. Yes No   Less than 5
    g. Yes No   Between 5 and 10
    h. Yes No   More than 10

    Average fiduciary audit experience of staff
    i. Yes No   None
    j. Yes No   Less than 3 years
    k. Yes No   Between 3 and 7 years
    l. Yes No   More than 7 years

20. Is the scope/frequency of the fiduciary audit based on:
    a. Yes No   Risk Matrix
    b. Yes No   Calendar

Company/Bank Name: _____

   c. Yes No   Combination of the above

   d. Yes No   Other (please describe)

                    _____

                    _____

                    _____

21. Trust audit reports are submitted to:
   a. Yes No   Board of Directors—Holding Company
   b. Yes No   Board of Directors—Bank or Trust Company
   c. Yes No   Trust Committee
   d. Yes No   Trust Audit Committee
   e. Yes No   CEO—Holding Company
   f. Yes No   CEO—Bank or Trust Company
   g. Yes No   Senior Trust Officers Committee
   h. Yes No   Senior Trust Officer
   i. Yes No   Other (please describe)

                    _____

                    _____

                    _____

22. Frequency of audit report to the Trust Audit Committee:
   a. Yes No   Monthly
   b. Yes No   Quarterly
   c. Yes No   Annually
   d. Yes No   Other (please describe)

                    _____

                    _____

                    _____

Company/Bank Name: _____

23. How does the Trust Audit Committee (TAC) determine that the scope of the fiduciary audits meets the institution's needs?
    a. Yes No   TAC independently reviews audit scope adequacy
    b. Yes No   TAC reviews trust audit scope with internal audit staff
    c. Yes No   CPA's or outside consultants are used to help determine fiduciary audit adequacy
    d. Yes No   Other (please describe)

    _____

    _____

    _____

24. Methods used to promote fiduciary legal/regulatory compliance include:
    a. Yes No   A fiduciary compliance officer is designated
    b. Yes No   Fiduciary compliance training program
    c. Yes No   Fiduciary compliance committee with representation from various functional areas
    d. Yes No   Compliance is specifically addressed in the performance appraisal system covering individual officers and employees
    e. Yes No   A process to identify and comply with new or changed requirements
    f. Yes No   Other (please describe)

    _____

    _____

    _____

25. Methods of Fiduciary Compliance Testing include:
    a. Yes No   Fiduciary compliance testing performed by trust auditor(s)

Company/Bank Name: _____

    b. Yes No   Fiduciary compliance testing performed by compliance officer(s)

    c. Yes No   Fiduciary compliance testing using peer reviews or self-assessments completed by trust officers

    d. Yes No   Fiduciary compliance testing is not performed

    e. Yes No   Other (please describe)

                    _____

                    _____

                    _____

26. What other factors can you describe that will help us understand how your institution identifies and manages fiduciary risks?

_____

_____

_____

_____

_____

_____

_____

NEW RISKS IN CORPORATE BOND TRUSTEE ADMINISTRATION

Corporate bond trustee relationships create very special concerns for the corporate fiduciary. They are highly complex and technical in nature and often are established under extensive legal review and documentation.

There are also statutory legal concerns that may pose risks to the corporate fiduciary. The most prevalent statute in this area is the Trust Indenture Act, TIA, of 1939 as amended by the Trust Indenture Reform Act, TIRA, of 1990 (enacted November 15, 1990). The TIA was enacted to protect unwary bond purchasers and bondholders from unscrupulous bond issuers, underwriters, promoters, etc., in the days shortly after the Great Depression, which ended in 1933. The TIA contains language under Section 310(b) which prohibits one from serving as a trustee under the bond in-

denture if there are certain types of "less than arms length" relationships among the issuer, underwriter, trustee, or any of their
affiliated companies or business interests.

DISQUALIFYING CONFLICTS OF INTEREST

Section 310(b) is known as the "Disqualifying Conflicts of Interest"
section of the TIA. Prior to amendments made through the TIRA,
the nine circumstances (subject to some technical exceptions and
limiting definitions) that would deem a trustee to have a disqualifying conflict of interest under the TIA are as follows:

1. If the trustee is also trustee under another indenture of the
   same issuer, except where the two issues are equal in class
   (not subordinated in that one gets priority payments over
   the other), and unsecured;
2. If the trustee or any of its directors or executive officers is
   an underwriter for an obligor on the indenture securities;
3. If the trustee is affiliated with such an obligor or an underwriter for such an obligor;
4. If the trustee or any of its directors or executive officers is a
   director, officer, partner, employee, appointee, or repre-
   sentative of such an obligor or an underwriter for such an
   obligor;
5. If 10% or more of the voting securities of the trustee is
   owned by such an obligor or any director, partner, or executive officer of the obligor (or 20% or more of such voting
   securities are owned by any two or more such persons; or
   10% or more of such voting securities of the trustee is
   owned by such underwriter and its directors, partners, and
   executive officers;
6. If the trustee owns 5% or more of the voting securities or
   10% or more of any other class of securities of such obligor
   or 10% or more of any class of securities of such underwriter;

7. If the trustee owns 5% or more of the voting securities of anyone affiliated with (or owning 10% or more of the voting securities of) such obligor;

8. If the trustee owns 10% or more of any class of securities of anyone owning 50% or more of the voting securities of such obligor; or

9. If the trustee holds for others 25% or more of any class of securities that would constitute a disqualifying conflict under (6), (7), or (8) above if such securities were "beneficially owned" by the trustee.

The TIRA added a tenth "Disqualifying Conflict" circumstance where the trustee is also a creditor of the obligor. On the surface, this appears to prohibit banks from serving as an indenture trustee while they are also a lender to the obligor.

However, the TIRA also changed the time at which the Section 310(b) conflicts disqualified the trustee. Under the TIA, the existence of a conflict at any time was sufficient to disqualify the trustee. The TIRA changed this time period to such time as "the indenture securities are in default (as such term is defined in the indenture), but exclusive of any period of grace or requirement of notice."

A trustee, therefore, assumes more risk during the administration of the trusteeship, but is freer to accept an appointment at inception since the trustee is not disqualified until the existence of a default. This obviously puts an imposing burden on the indenture trustee to determine the existence of any such default.

> (Note: There is one disqualifying conflict that remains intact at ALL TIMES. This is a new Section 310(a)(5) which prohibits an obligor or its affiliates from serving as its OWN trustee upon the indenture securities.)

The TIRA contains provisions that can help the trustee to avoid resignations in the event of a minor or technical default; it cannot be a payment default. The trustee must file an application with the SEC for an order finding that the default "may be cured or waived during a reasonable period under procedures specified in the application" and that the nonresignation of the trustee "will not be inconsistent with the interests of the holders of the indenture securities."

CONTRACTUAL VERSUS FIDUCIARY OBLIGATIONS OF TRUSTEE

The change in verbiage from "...at any time..." to "...in default..." to define the disqualifying period is consistent with the banking industry's notion (upheld in various court cases) that the bond trustee's "predefault" role is contractual in nature and not similar to the high degree of fiduciary responsibilities afforded a common law trustee. Often acting as receiving agent of securities, paying agent for interest and principal, transfer agent, etc., the bond trustee under TIRA seems to assume only ministerial responsibilities prior to default.

Banks that underwrite securities will, therefore, be allowed to also function as indenture trustee under TIRA until a default takes place. Further, underwriters will be able to create affiliates chartered as trust companies who can act as indenture trustee until a default exists. Since TIRA advocates an interpretation of contractual rather than fiduciary duties prior to a default, less than arms length parties can participate. (Please note that the inherent risk from litigation in this activity is not substantially lessened. Where previously a bondholder could bring suit claiming a breach of fiduciary duty under the Trust Indenture Act of 1939, the same bondholder could now use, e.g., RICO as the federal statute if the bondholder claimed he or she was damaged due to racketeering or conspiracy between such "less than arms length" parties.)

Also, there becomes a very risky situation upon default. A trustee who had not previously resigned a troubled issuer trusteeship prior to default will be immediately obligated to protect bondholders as a prudent man would protect his or her own property while the conflict exists, until a successor trustee is appointed and accepts appointment.

It seems clear that one of TIRA's intents is to widen the availability of indenture trustees for bond offerings. One of the consequences is to put the burden on the trustee to keenly monitor for default warning signals and to resign prior to (although not required by TIRA) the actual default. An ancillary problem is the capability of the resigning trustee to secure a successor trustee, since the resigning trustee cannot resign until the successor is appointed and accepts.

OTHER ASPECTS OF TIRA THAT COULD POSE PROBLEMS

Previously, under TIA most of Sections 310 through 317 included the phrase "...the indenture to be qualified shall provide that...". Therefore, there was usually about 25 or 30 pages of boilerplate provisions in every indenture. TIRA attempts to eliminate this boilerplate in the indentures by using the phrase "...The Trustee shall...". **The previously boilerplate provisions in the indenture are now superseded by federal law.**

Therefore, to include any of the old boilerplate provisions in the indenture could be potentially confusing for compliance, especially if there is inconsistency in the TIRA provisions. **The boilerplate provisions will probably have to be carried to the prospectus to the extent they are necessary to describe the securities under federal securities laws. Review of the prospectus with the TIRA required provisions would then become necessary.**

Because these provisions are now part of federal law, there are now POTENTIALLY DRASTIC CONSEQUENCES in noncompliance. Previously, trustees would consider their duties in the context of potential civil litigation for breach of contract. Now, violations are subject to CRIMINAL SANCTIONS under

Section 325 of the TIA. Combined with the SEC's new enforcement powers under the Securities Enforcement Remedies and Penny Stock Reform Act of 1990, this new context could become a dangerous weapon against the trustee or officer of the trustee who fails to perform even the most insignificant duty under these previously boilerplate provisions. Further, the TIRA makes these provisions retroactive to existing qualified indenture securities.

It is clear that the issuers and trustees will need to create comprehensive policies and procedures to help ensure that they do not fail to comply with what were previously contractual obligations as the risks from such noncompliance now are greatly increased.

TRUSTEE REPORTING CHANGES

The TIA of 1939 required trustees to report annually to bondholders regarding the following:

1. The trustee's continued eligibility as trustee;
2. The nature and amount of advances made to the obligor;
3. Any indebtedness by the obligor to the bank as individual;
4. Property and funds in the trustee's possession;
5. Trustee releases of collateral;
6. Additional issuance of indenture securities by obligor;
7. Any trustee action which materially affects bondholders.

The TIRA amends this so that the trustee is only required to report to the bondholders to the extent a change has occurred in the previous 12 months. Therefore, **nonreporting should be supported by evidence of the status quo.**

The TIRA also adds a reporting requirement upon the obligor. **The obligor is now required by federal law to furnish the trustee, at least annually, an authorized certificate that the obligor is complying with all conditions and covenants under the indenture.** This information is extremely important now that disqualification of the trustee with a conflict only takes place upon default. It gives the trustee a **statutory early warning system** for violations of indenture covenants.

Competitive and conforming aspects of the TIRA include the following: 1) allowing foreign corporations to act as indenture trustees under TIRA if reciprocal laws exist in the trustee's domicile; 2) allowing bondholder consent solicitations more time to make DTC-held bonds more suitable in the time frames the consent solicitations are required for; and 3) the period for sharing of recoveries with bondholders with regard to preferential claims being shortened from four months to three months to conform with the Bankruptcy Reform Act of 1978.

CREDIT RATINGS OF FIXED INCOME AND MONEY MARKET SECURITIES

KEY TO STANDARD & POOR'S CORPORATE AND MUNICIPAL BOND RATING DEFINITIONS

Standard & Poor's corporate or municipal debt rating is a current assessment of the creditworthiness of an obligor with respect to a specific debt obligation. This assessment may take into consideration obligors such as guarantors, insurers, or lessees.

The debt rating is not a recommendation to purchase, sell, or hold a security, inasmuch as it does not comment as to market price or suitability for a particular investor.

The ratings are based on current information furnished by the issuer or obtained by Standard & Poor's from other sources it considers reliable. Standard & Poor's does not perform an audit in connection with any rating and may, on occasion, rely on un-audited financial information. The ratings may be changed due to changes in, or unavailability of, such information, or for other circumstances.

The ratings are based, in varying degrees, on the following considerations:

1. Likelihood of default—capacity and willingness of the obligor as to the timely payment of interest and repayment of principal in accordance with the terms of the obligation;
2. Nature of and provisions of the obligation;
3. Protection afforded by, and relative position of, the obligation in the event of bankruptcy, reorganization, or other arrangement under the laws of bankruptcy and other laws affecting creditor's rights.

Standard & Poor's Debt Ratings

AAA

Debt rated **AAA** have the highest rating assigned by Standard & Poor's to a debt obligation. Capacity to pay interest and repay principal is extremely strong.

AA

Debt rated **AA** have a very strong capacity to pay interest and repay principal and differ from the highest rated issues only to a small degree.

A

Debt rated **A** have a strong capacity to pay interest and repay principal, although they are somewhat more susceptible to the adverse effects of changes in circumstances and economic conditions than debts in higher rated categories.

BBB

Debt rated **BBB** are regarded as having an adequate capacity to pay interest and repay principal. Whereas they normally exhibit adequate protection parameters, adverse economic conditions or changing circumstances are more likely to lead to a weakened capacity to pay interest and repay principal for debts in this category than for debts in higher rated categories.

BB, B, CCC, CC

Debt rated **BB, B, CCC,** and **CC** are regarded, on balance, as predominantly speculative with respect to capacity to pay interest and repay interest and repay principal in accordance with the terms of the obligation. **BB** indicates the lowest degree of speculation and **CC** the highest degree of speculation. While such debts will likely have some quality and protective characteristics, these are outweighed by large uncertainties or major risk exposures to adverse conditions.

C

The rating **C** is reserved for income bonds on which no interest is being paid.

D

Debt rated **D** are in default, and payment of interest and/or repayment of principal is in arrears.

Plus (+) or minus (-)

The ratings from **AA** to **B** may be modified by the addition of a plus or minus sign to show relative standing within the major rating categories.

Provisional ratings

The letter "p" indicates that the rating is provisional. A provisional rating assumes the successful completion of the project being financed by the debts being rated and indicates that payment of debt service requirements is largely or entirely dependent upon the successful and timely completion of the project. This rating, however, while addressing credit quality subsequent to completion of the project, makes no comment on the likelihood of, or risk of default upon failure of such completion. The investor should exercise his or her own judgment with respect to such likelihood and risk.

L

The letter "L" indicates that the rating pertains to the principal amount of those bonds where the underlying deposit collateral is fully insured by the Federal Savings & Loan Insurance Corp. or the Federal Deposit Insurance Corp.

NR

Indicates that no rating has been requested, that there is insufficient information on which to base a rating, or that S&P does not rate a particular type of obligation as a matter of policy.

Debt Obligations

Debt obligations of issuers outside the United States and its territories are rated on the same basis as domestic, corporate, and municipal issues. The ratings measure the creditworthiness of the obligor but do not take into account currency exchange and other uncertainties.

Bond Investment Quality Standards

Under present commercial bank regulations issued by the Comptroller of the Currency, bonds rated in the top four categories (AAA, AA, A, BBB, commonly known as "Investment Grade" ratings) are generally regarded as eligible for bank investment. In addition, the legal investment laws of various states impose certain ratings or other standards for obligations eligible for investment by savings banks, trust companies, insurance companies, and fiduciaries.

KEY TO STANDARD & POOR'S PREFERRED STOCK RATING DEFINITIONS

A Standard & Poor's preferred stock rating is an assessment of the capacity and willingness of an issuer to pay preferred stock dividends and any applicable sinking fund obligations. A preferred stock rating differs from a bond rating inasmuch as it is assigned to an equity issue, which issue is intrinsically different from, and subordinated to, a debt issue. Therefore, to reflect this difference, the preferred stock rating symbol will normally not be higher than the bond rating symbol assigned to, or that would be assigned to, the senior debt of the same issuer.

The preferred stock ratings are based on the following considerations:

1. Likelihood of payment—capacity and willingness of the issuer to meet the timely payment of preferred stock dividends and any applicable sinking fund requirements in accordance with the terms of the obligation;
2. Nature of and provisions of the issue;
3. Relative position of the issue in the event of bankruptcy, reorganization, or other arrangements affecting creditor's rights;

Standard & Poor's Preferred Stock Ratings

AAA

The highest rating that may be assigned by Standard & Poor's to a preferred stock issue and indicates an extremely strong capacity to pay the preferred stock obligations.

AA

A preferred stock issue rated **AA** also qualifies as a high-quality fixed income security. The capacity to pay preferred stock obligations is very strong, although not as overwhelming as for issues rated **AAA**.

A

An issue rated **A** is backed by a sound capacity to pay the preferred stock obligations, although it is somewhat more susceptible to the adverse effects of changes in circumstances and economic conditions.

BBB

An issue rated **BBB** is regarded as backed by adequate capacity to pay the preferred stock obligation. Whereas it normally exhibits adequate protection parameters, adverse economic conditions or changing circumstances are more likely to lead to a weakened capacity to make payments for a preferred stock in this category than for issues in the **A** category.

BB, B, CCC

Preferred stock rated **BB, B,** and **CCC** are regarded, on balance, as predominantly speculative with respect to the issuer's capacity to pay preferred stock obligations. **BB** indicates the lowest degree of speculation and **CCC** the highest degree of speculation. While such issues will likely have some quality and protective characteristics, these are outweighed by large uncertainties or major risk exposures to adverse conditions.

CC

The rating **CC** is reserved for a preferred stock issue in arrears on dividends or sinking fund payments, but one that is currently paying.

C

A preferred stock rated **C** is a nonpaying issue.

D

A preferred stock rated **D** is a nonpaying issue with the issuer in default on debt instruments.

NR

NR indicates that no rating has been requested, that there is insufficient information on which to base a rating, or that S&P does not rate a particular type of obligation as a matter or policy.

Plus (+) or Minus (-)

To provide more detailed indications of preferred stock quality, the ratings from **AA** to **B** may be modified by the addition of a plus or minus sign to show relative standing within the major rating categories.

The preferred stock rating is not a recommendation to purchase or sell a security, inasmuch as market price is not considered in arriving at the rating. Preferred stock ratings are wholly unrelated to Standard & Poor's earnings and dividend rankings for common stocks.

Municipal Notes

A Standard & Poor's role rating reflects the liquidity concerns and market access risks unique to notes. Notes due in three years or less will likely receive a long-term debt rating. The following criteria will be used in making that assessment:

- Amortization schedule (the larger the final maturity relative to other maturities the more likely it will be treated as a note);

- Source of payment (the more dependent the issue is on the market for its refinancing, the more likely it will be treated as a note).

Note rating symbols are as follows:

SP-1 Very strong or strong capacity to pay principal and interest. Those issues determined to possess overwhelming safety characteristics will be given a plus (+) designation;

SP-2 Satisfactory capacity to pay principal and interest;

SP-3 Speculative capacity to pay principal and interest.

Tax-Exempt Demand Bonds

Standard & Poor's assigns "dual" ratings to all long-term debt issues that have as part of their provisions a demand or double feature.

The first rating addresses the likelihood of repayment of principal and interest as due, and the second rating addresses only the demand feature. The long-term debt rating symbols are used for bonds to denote the long-term maturity, and the commercial paper rating symbols are used to denote the put option (for example, "AAA/A-1+"). For the newer "demand notes," S&P's note rating symbols, combined with the commercial paper symbols, are used (for example, "SP-1+/A-1+").

KEY TO STANDARD & POOR'S
COMMERCIAL PAPER RATING DEFINITIONS

A Standard & Poor's Commercial Paper Rating is a current assessment of the likelihood of timely payment of debt having an original maturity of no more than 365 days.

Ratings are graded into four categories, ranging from A for the highest quality obligations to D for the lowest. The four categories are as follows:

A

Issues assigned this highest rating are regarded as having the greatest capacity for timely payment of debt having an original maturity of no more than 365 days.

The **As** are further divided into three categories as follows:

A-1   This designation indicates that the degree of safety regarding timely payment is very strong.

A-2   Capacity for timely payment on issues with this designation is strong. However, the relative degree of safety is not as overwhelming as for issues designated A-1.

A-3   Issues carrying this designation have a satisfactory capacity for timely payment. They are, however, somewhat more vulnerable to the adverse effects of changes in circumstances than obligations carrying the higher designations.

B

Issues rated **B** are regarded as having only an adequate capacity for timely payment. However, such capacity may be damaged by changing conditions for short-term adversities.

C

This rating is assigned to short-term obligations with doubtful capacity for payment.

D

This rating indicates that the issue is either in default or is expected to be in default upon maturity.

The Commercial Paper Rating is not a recommendation to purchase or sell a security. The ratings are based on current information furnished to Standard & Poor's by the issuer or obtained from other sources it considers reliable. The ratings may be changed, suspended, or withdrawn as a result of changes in, or unavailability of, such information.

KEY TO MOODY'S MUNICIPAL RATINGS

Aaa

Bonds which are rated **Aaa** are judged to be of the best quality. They carry the smallest degree of investment risk and are generally referred to as "gilt edge." Interest payments are protected by a large or by an exceptionally stable margin, and principal is secure. While the various protective elements are likely to change, such changes that can be visualized are most unlikely to impair the fundamentally strong position of such issues.

Aa

Bonds which are rated **Aa** are judged to be of high quality by all standards. Together with the **Aaa** group they makeup what are generally known as high grade bonds. They are rated lower than the best bonds because margins of protection may not be as large as in **Aaa** securities fluctuation of protective elements present may be of greater amplitude, or there may be other elements present which make the long-term risks appear somewhat larger than in **Aaa** securities.

A

Bonds which are rated **A** possess many favorable investment attributes and are to be considered as upper-medium-grade obligations. Factors giving security to principal and interest are considered adequate, but elements may be present which suggest a susceptibility to impairment sometime in the future.

Baa

Bonds which are rated **Baa** are considered as medium grade obligations; i.e., they are neither highly protected nor poorly secured. Interest payments and principal security appear adequate for the present, but certain protective elements may be lacking or may be characteristically unreliable over any great length of time. Such bonds lack outstanding investment characteristics and in fact have speculative characteristics as well.

Ba

Bonds rated **Ba** are judged to have speculative elements; their future cannot be considered as well assured. Often the protection of interest and principal payments may be very moderate, and thereby not well safeguarded during both good and bad times over the future. Uncertainty of position characterizes bonds in this case.

B

Bonds rated **B** generally lack characteristics of the desirable investment. Assurance of interest and principal payments or of maintenance of other terms of the contract over any long period of time may be small.

Caa

Bonds rated **Caa** are of poor standing. Such issues may be in default or there may be present elements of danger with respect to principal or interest.

Ca

Bonds rated **Ca** represent obligations which are speculative in a high degree. Such issues are often in default or have other marked shortcomings.

C

Bonds rated **C** are the lowest rated class of bonds, and issues so rated can be regarded as having extremely poor prospects of ever attaining any real investment standing.

Con.(-)

Bonds for which the security depends upon the completion of some act or the fulfillment of some condition are rated conditionally. These are bonds secured by: (a) earnings of projects under construction, (b) earnings of projects unseasoned in operation experience, (c) rentals which begin when facilities are completed, or (d) payments to which some other limiting condition attaches. Parenthetical rating denotes probable credit stature upon completion of construction or elimination of basis of condition.

KEY TO MOODY'S CORPORATE RATINGS

Aaa

Bonds rated **Aaa** are judged to be best quality. They carry the smallest degree of investment risk and are generally referred to as "gilt edge." Interest payments are protected by a large or by an exceptionally stable margin and principal is secure. While the various protective elements are likely to change, such changes that can be visualized are most unlikely to impair the fundamentally strong position of such issues.

Aa

Bonds rated **Aa** are judged to be of high quality by all standards. Together with the **Aaa** group they compose what are generally known as high grade bonds. They are rated lower than the best bonds because margins of protection may not be as large as in **Aaa** securities, fluctuation of protective elements may be of greater amplitude, or there may be other elements present which make the long-term risks appear somewhat larger than in **Aaa** securities.

A

Bonds rated **A** possess many favorable investment attributes and are considered as upper-medium-grade obligations. Factors giving security to principal and interest are considered adequate, but elements may be present which suggest a susceptibility to impairment sometime in the future.

Baa

Bonds rated Baa are considered as medium grade obligations, i.e., they are neither highly protected nor poorly secured. Interest payments and principal security appear adequate for the present, but certain protective elements may be lacking or may be characteristically unreliable over any great length of time. Such bonds lack outstanding investment characteristics and in fact have speculative characteristics as well.

Ba

Bonds rated Ba are judged to have a speculative element; their future cannot be considered as well assured. Often the protection of interest and principal payments may be very moderate and thereby not well safeguarded during both good and bad times over the future. Uncertainty of position characterizes bonds in this class.

B

Bonds rated **B** generally lack characteristics of the desirable investment. Assurance of interest and principal payments or of maintenance of other terms of the contract over any long period of time may be small.

Caa

Bonds rated **Caa** are of poor standing. Such issues may be in default or there may be present elements of danger with respect to principal or interest.

Ca

Bonds rated **Ca** represent obligations which are speculative in a high degree. Such issues are often in default or have other marked shortcomings.

C

Bonds rated **C** are the lowest rated class of bonds and issues so rated can be regarded as having extremely poor prospects of ever attaining any real investment standing.

KEY TO MOODY'S COMMERCIAL PAPER RATINGS

The term "commercial paper" as used by Moody's means promissory obligations not having an original maturity in excess of nine months. Moody's makes no representation as to whether such commercial paper is by any other definition "commercial paper" or is exempt from registration under the Securities Act of 1933, as amended.

Moody's Commercial Paper ratings are opinions of the ability of issuers to repay punctually promissory obligations, not having an original maturity in excess of nine months. Moody's makes no representation that such obligations are exempt from registration under Securities Act of 1933, nor does it represent that any specific note is a valid obligation of a rated issuer or is issued in conformity with any applicable law. Moody's employs the following three designations, all judged to be investment grade, to indicate the relative repayment capacity of rated issuers:

- Issuers rated **"Prime-1"** (or related supporting institutions) have a superior capacity for repayment of short-term promissory obligations. Prime-1 repayment capacity will normally be evidenced by the following characteristics:

  - Leading market positions in well-established industries.

  - High rates of return on funds employed.

  - Conservative capitalization structures with moderate reliance on debt and ample asset protection.

  - Broad margins in earnings coverage of fixed financial charges and high internal cash generations.

  - Well-established access to a range of financial markets and assured sources of alternate liquidity.

- Issuers rated **"Prime-2"** (or related supporting institutions) have a strong capacity for short-term promissory obligations. This will normally be evidenced by many of the characteristics cited above but to a lesser degree.

Earnings trends and coverage ratios, while sound, will be more subject to variation. Capitalization characteristics, while still appropriate, may be more affected by external conditions. Ample alternate liquidity is maintained.

- Issuers rated **"Prime-3"** (or related supporting institutions) have an acceptable capacity for repayment of short-term promissory obligations. The effect of industry characteristics and market composition may be more pronounced. Variability in earnings and profitability may result in changes in the level of debt protection measurements and the requirement for relatively high financial leverage. Adequate liquidity is maintained.

- Issuers rated **"Not Prime"** do not fall within any of the Prime rating categories.

If an issuer represents to Moody's that its commercial paper obligations are supported by the credit of another entity or entities, the name or names of such supporting entity or entities are listed within parenthesis beneath the name of the issuer. In assigning ratings to such issuers, Moody's evaluates the financial strength of the indicated affiliated corporations, commercial banks, insurance companies, foreign governments, or other entities, but only as one factor in the total rating assessment. Moody's makes no representation and gives no opinion on the legal validity or enforceability of any support arrangement. You are cautioned to review any questions regarding particular support arrangements with your own counsel.

KEY TO MOODY'S PREFERRED STOCK RATINGS

Moody's Rating Policy Review Board extended its rating services to include quality designations on preferred stocks on October 1, 1973. The decision to rate preferred stocks, which Moody's had done prior to 1935, was prompted by evidence of investor interest.

Moody's believes that its rating of preferred stocks is especially appropriate in view of the ever-increasing amount of these securities outstanding, and the fact that continuing inflation and its ramifications have resulted generally in the dilution of some of the protection afforded them as well as other fixed-income securities.

Because of the fundamental differences between preferred stocks and bonds, a variation of our familiar bond rating symbols is being used in the quality ranking of preferred stocks. The symbols, presented below, are designed to avoid comparison with bond quality in absolute terms. It should always be borne in mind that preferred stocks occupy a junior position to bonds within a particular capital structure.

Preferred stock rating symbols and their definitions are as follows:

aaa

An issue which is rated **aaa** is considered to be a top-quality preferred stock. This rating indicates good asset protection and the least risk of dividend impairment within the universe of preferred stocks.

aa

An issue which is rated **aa** is considered a high-grade preferred stock. This rating indicates that there is a reasonable assurance that earnings and asset protection will remain relatively well maintained in the foreseeable future.

a

An issue which is rated **a** is considered to be upper-mediu-grade preferred stock. While risks are judged to be somewhat greater than in the "**aaa**" and "**aa**" classifications, earnings and asset protection are, nevertheless, expected to be maintained at adequate levels.

baa

An issue which is rated **baa** is considered to be medium grade, neither highly protected nor poorly secured. Earnings and asset protection appear adequate at present but may be questionable over any length of time.

ba

An issue which is rated **ba** is considered to have speculative elements and its future cannot be considered well assured. Earnings and asset protection may be very moderate and not well safeguarded during adverse periods. Uncertainty of position characterizes preferred stocks in this class.

b

An issue rated **b** generally lacks the characteristics of a desirable investment. Assurance of dividend payment and maintenance of other terms of the issue over any long period of time may be small.

caa

An issue which is rated **caa** is likely to be in arrears on dividend payments. This rating designation does not purport to indicate the future status of payments.

ca

An issue which is rated **ca** is speculative in a high degree and is likely to be in arrears on dividends with little likelihood of eventual payment.

c

This is the lowest rated class of preferred or preference stock. Issues rated as such can be regarded as having extremely poor prospects of ever attaining any real investment standing.

KEY TO SHORT-TERM LOAN RATINGS

MIG 1/VMIG 1

This designation denotes best quality. There is present strong protection by established cash flows, superior liquidity support or demonstrated broadbased access to the market for refinancing. MIG

MIG 2/VMIG 2

This designation denotes high quality. Margins of protection are ample although not so large as in the preceding group.

MIG 3/VMIG 3

This designation denotes favorable quality. All security elements are accounted for, but there lacks the undeniable strength of the preceding grades. Liquidity and cash flow protection may be narrow and market access for refinancing is likely to be less well established.

MIG 4/VMIG 4

This designation denotes adequate quality. Protection commonly regarded as required of an investment security is present and although not distinctly or predominantly speculative, there is specific risk.

Issues or the features associated with MIG or VMIG ratings are identified by date of issue, date of maturity or maturities, or rating expiration date and description to distinguish each rating from other ratings. Each rating designation is unique with no implication as to any other issue of the same obligor. MIG ratings terminate at the retirement of the obligation while VMIG rating expiration will be a function of each issue's specific structural or credit features.

FIDUCIARY POLICIES RECOMMENDED BY OFFICE OF THE COMPTROLLER OF THE CURRENCY— MIDWEST DISTRICT

REQUIRED POLICIES

1. 12CFR9.5—Brokerage Placement Practices.

2. 12CFR9.7(D)—Use of Material Inside Information.

3. 12CFR9.10(A)—Cash Management Practices.

4. 12CFR12.6—Securities Trading Policies.

POLICIES STRONGLY RECOMMENDED FOR SAFETY AND SOUNDNESS OF INVESTMENTS

5. Investment purchase and retention policies, including policies that govern the required account and issuer reviews under 12CFR9.7.
6. Portfolio management and asset allocation policies.
7. Proxy voting policies.
8. Policies governing acceptance and administration of accounts containing closely held businesses, limited partnerships, real estate, real estate mortgages, mineral interests, or other miscellaneous assets as investments.
9. Policies governing acceptance of general partnership interests as investments.
10. Qualification policies for persons performing real estate appraisals.
11. Policies providing criteria for the retention of investments which are recommended as "sells."

CONFLICTS OF INTEREST

12. Policies governing purchase, sale and retention of bank stock, and other obligations.
13. Policies governing transactions with directors, officers, employees, or other parties (and their interests) with whom there may exist a relationship that may impair the best judgment of the trustee in acting in the best interests of the beneficiaries.
14. Investment policies regarding investment in firms selling property or supplies to the bank.
15. Policies over loans, repurchase agreements, and other assets purchased from the bank or its affiliates.

16. Policies governing loans from the bank to trust accounts and the taking of collateral from the trust.
17. Investment policies for the purchase of securities from syndicates in which the bank or its affiliates participate.
18. Dual relationship policies where the bank is both creditor and bond trustee for the company.
19. Policies for fairness in the cross selling of assets between accounts.
20. Policies governing the acceptance of financial benefits from investment management companies, service companies, etc.
21. Policies governing transactions such as loans to closely held businesses held in trust.
22. General conflict of interest policies.

ETHICS AND PERSONNEL POLICIES

23. Fiduciary code of ethics.
24. Treatment of confidential information.
25. Relationship with co-fiduciaries, beneficiaries, and settlors of trust.
26. Bank officers and employees serving as directors of outside concerns.
27. Bank officers and employees serving as co-fiduciaries.
28. Acceptance of gifts or legacies by officers and employees.
29. Relationships with professional groups.
30. General personnel policies.

GENERAL POLICIES

31. Environmental cleanup liabilities.
32. Acceptance and termination of accounts.
33. Acceptance of successor trusteeships.

34. Discretionary payments from fiduciary accounts.
35. Joint custody and dual control over fiduciary assets.
36. Internal controls.
37. Audit coverage for fiduciary activities.
38. Litigation.
39. Customer complaints.
40. Compensation for fiduciary services and fee concessions.
41. Fiduciary marketing policies.
42. Control and use of suspense accounts.
43. Escheat.
44. Chargeoffs.
45. Overdrafts in fiduciary accounts.
46. Accounting statements to fiduciary customers.
47. Written approval and authorization from co-fiduciaries.
48. Written direction from outside powerholders.
49. Communication with fiduciary customers.
50. Fiduciary account file documentation.
51. Record retention.
52. Pledging for fiduciary deposits.
53. Guarantees.
54. Nominee registration.
55. Maintenance of will file.

INDEX